HEAD TRAUMA

HEAD TRAUMA

The Bruising Diary
of a Headteacher

NICK SMITH

Michael O'Mara Books Limited

First published in Great Britain in 2022 by
Michael O'Mara Books Limited
9 Lion Yard
Tremadoc Road
London SW4 7NQ

A CIP catalogue record for this book is available from the British Library.

Papers used by Michael O'Mara Books Limited are natural, recyclable products made
from wood grown in sustainable forests. The manufacturing processes conform to the
environmental regulations of the country of origin.

ISBN: 978-1-78929-369-2 in hardback print format
ISBN: 978-1-78929-414-9 in ebook format

1 2 3 4 5 6 7 8 9 10

Every reasonable effort has been made to contact all parties mentioned in this work. Any
errors or omissions that may have occurred are inadvertent, and anyone with any queries
is invited to write to the publisher, so that a full acknowledgement may be included
in subsequent editions of this work. In some instances, names and context have been
changed and abridged to protect the identity of the individual, and occasionally the
author has created a fictionalized character, inspired by a range of individuals, in order
to protect their identities.

Typeset by Natasha LeCoultre and Julyan Bayes

www.mombooks.com

To my wife, sweet Caroline

Contents

PART THREE: CLIMBING THE GREASY POLE

PART FOUR: HEADSHIP I: THE COMPLIANT YEARS

PART FIVE: HEADSHIP II: THE BELLIGERENT YEARS

Acknowledgements

I owe a huge debt of gratitude to all the students, parents, staff and governors who have provided me with the many, and sometimes difficult, lessons in leadership. I am much indebted to Paul Bourdeaux whose inspirational guidance set me off on my journey and, similarly, I would like to thank my good friend James Gregory for supporting me every step of the way.

I would particularly like to thank the ten headteachers of the Southwest Academic Trust, whose support, comradeship and humour over many years has never failed to raise my spirits and helped to lessen the loneliness that can come with headship.

Many thanks to my agent Katie Fulford for her faith, and my editor Nicki Crossley for her brilliantly astute observations. Finally, I am grateful to my family for putting up with this cantankerous old fool for so long, and above all else, I have treasured the support of my remarkable wife, Caroline.

Introduction

After five ambivalent years at medical school, I graduated in 1988 undecided whether a career in medicine was for me. Eighteen months working as a junior doctor helped bring some much-needed clarity to my thinking: it was definitely not for me. I had neither the passion nor the resolve essential to survive in the NHS, and therefore, amid one cry of 'That's a shame, you'll be missed' from one rather confused patient, but many more from the nursing staff announcing, 'He's gone, it's safe to return to your beds', I boldly left.

This audacious move lost its shine almost immediately because, despite a smattering of supportive comments from friends and family, it was clear that most people thought I had lost my marbles. My mother, who had been a nurse all her working life, found my decision to give up completely unfathomable. As a single parent it had been a struggle bringing up two spirited boys, so she had consequently been ridiculously proud when I became the first in the family to go to university, and then go on to qualify as a doctor. When I nervously popped round to break the news, her disappointment was palpable and contributed to the growing feeling that I had let everybody, including myself, down.

With her parting reproach, 'You are throwing away your chance to do something really meaningful' ringing in my ears, I found myself desperately looking around for an alternative career that would help re-establish my credibility. So it was in 1990 – against the backdrop of the Gulf War, the birth of the internet and at the end of Nelson Mandela's long road to freedom – that I decided to give another public service the benefit of my untapped genius. I applied to train as a teacher. I reasoned that education had to be easier than medicine. There would be no bodily fluids, there would be endless work-free holidays, and the students would find me considerably hipper than the other teachers because I wore Dr Martens. Sadly, I was wrong on all counts, and particularly the one about being hip.

However, having now decided that teaching would be my road to redemption, I dared to dream expansively about my new calling. I envisaged delivering lessons so intensely stimulating that in the future students would go misty-eyed as they fondly remembered me as the teacher who had inspired them. I saw other teachers pleading with me to mentor their difficult students because, somehow, I had the knack of getting through to troubled teenagers. I did not let my imagination stop there. Why not go the whole hog and become a headteacher, I reasoned? Not just any old headteacher either, but the type of headteacher who could galvanize and inspire a generation of students. A charismatic headteacher whose rousing assemblies would have students out of their seats clamouring for more. One for whom staff would go over the top; a leader who had the touch. Surely if I were to achieve such heroic headteacher status my salvation would be complete?

Well, it seemed a laudable plan at the time, but as I began my teacher training I was unaware of what awaited me. I had entered another pressurized profession, but it was one that did not enjoy quite the same love and respect as medicine. It was like jumping off the *Titanic* only to be rescued by the *Costa Concordia*.

Three decades and seven schools later, I am a soon-to-retire head of a state secondary school. On the wall in my office is a children's toy, a plastic monster's head which, if pressed, emits a pre-recorded message. The message is, 'it beggars belief', and it is my favourite and most frequently used expression. I press the monster whenever I, pupils, parents, staff or the Department of Education (DfE) do something that is notable, ludicrous, odd, bewildering or unreasonable. It is pressed so often that I am forever having to replace the batteries.

I have gathered together in this diary a collection of the key incidents that over the past thirty years have demanded a press of the monster. The incidents range from my embarrassing assembly on how much sex everyone was having, to the ridiculous 2020 exam grade fiasco. Collectively they illustrate the daily grind of life at the whiteboard face in UK schools. They may go some way towards explaining why teachers grumble so much, are fiercely defensive of their long holidays, and in particular why it is not so easy to become a 'Hero Head'. If not, the least they will do is show how the trauma of school life can, so often, beggar belief.

Nick Smith

Part One: In Training

JANUARY 1991:

THE ZOO

After laying down my stethoscope I had eight months to wait until my teacher training course began, so I sought some suitable employment to tide me over. I was fortunate enough to land a job at London Zoo, looking after the diving birds. The undisputed superstars of my section were the penguins and, charmed by their endearing appearance and jaunty nature, I looked forward to caring for them. How curious that it would be here, in the zoo's iconic penguin pool, that I would learn the rudiments of classroom management.

The penguins were as good as gold when their usual keeper was present, but as soon as I was on my own, they turned on me. On entering the pool, the whole jabbering pack would surround me, and I would be subjected to a sustained pecking assault. They would peck at my hands and legs, demanding food and attention. It was all I could do not to run, yelp or shove them hard into the water.

Unfortunately, none of these were options because the pool was constantly surrounded by visitors cooing and giggling at their madcap antics. To top it all, much of my day involved cleaning up excrement. On the positive side, by the time I left, my future classroom management skills had developed considerably. I had acquired a sixth sense and a third eye, so I could identify the troublemakers at twenty paces. I could distract them from their pecking and get them to follow me in a semi-orderly fashion. Sadly, I never gained any control over their bowels.

This experience came in handy when I spent a week in a primary reception class, a prerequisite for my course. Here, the adorable five-year-olds were as good as gold when their usual teacher was present but, as soon as I was on my own, they turned on me. On entering the classroom, the whole jabbering pack would surround me, and I would be subjected to a sustained pecking assault. They would peck at my hands and legs, demanding food and attention. It was all I could do not to run, yelp or shove them hard under a desk. Unfortunately, none of these were options because the classroom was often surrounded by parents cooing and giggling at their madcap antics. To top all of this, my day also involved cleaning up excrement. However, I was thankful for my time at the zoo because my penguin-taming skills meant that my week with the reception class was bearable. On reflection, I was also thankful that I had chosen secondary teaching because the constant attention required by smaller children, and the unnerving thought of being stuck with the same gremlins all day, every day for a whole year, was frightening. However, I had already gained enormous respect for the resilience shown by my primary colleagues in the face of unremitting demand and continuous defecation.

SEPTEMBER 1991:
THE PECKING ORDER

In September 1991, my girlfriend Caroline and I began our teacher training courses at a London teacher training college. She was training to be a primary school teacher and I was training to teach secondary science. Because of the severe shortage of science graduates who believed teaching to be a good career choice, my course came with a £600 golden handshake. As I filled out the application form, I remember thinking just how much money all those other graduates were missing out on. They, meanwhile, were busily filling out job applications that would provide them with at least £600 more than me – every month – for the rest of their working lives.

There were six students in my tutorial group. Apart from me, three others were also mature students: a marketing executive, a German PhD graduate and an ebullient city accountant called Huxley, with whom I bonded immediately.

The other two were younger students who had just finished their first degrees, neither of whom actually wanted to be teachers, but they were keen to continue living a student lifestyle and couldn't think of anything better to do. We were without doubt a motley crew and I imagined that we were some way off the committed, high-calibre field the government was hoping to attract. Our university tutor was a diminutive academic called Dr Maitland. Softly spoken, she wore home-knitted jumpers covered in cat hair and smelt of musty old books. She spent most of our tutorials endlessly waffling on about theories of learning, and we strongly suspected it had been many decades since she had last taught a live lesson.

Our course kicked off with several weeks of lectures and tutorials, the content of which, for the life of me, I cannot recall but they were essentially the warm-up for the main event: our teaching placements. As we approached the point at which we were to be released into the wild, there was a growing sense of unease among the trainees. This was partly fuelled by the realisation that our untried teaching prowess was about to be tested and partly fuelled by the placement horror stories that were merrily circulating. Have you heard about the trainee whose class locked him in a cupboard/ set fire to the lab/stole his trousers/made him cry/put him in a coma? And any number of other scenarios involving severe embarrassment and/or physical pain. I brushed these fears aside because I knew it would be different for me.

I understood teenagers; why, I had been one myself only recently. 'Talk to the hand', 'whatever', 'not'. See, I spoke their language. They wouldn't behave like that for me. Would they? As D-Day approached, I found myself favouring a comfortable school in a leafy suburb.

The boys' school I was assigned to was indeed in a suburb, but it lacked both comfort and leaves. To describe it as an academic powerhouse would be a big fat lie, as well as an insult to powerhouses everywhere. This was London in the '90s, and if students or staff could get into a well-funded, grant-maintained school, then they did. Everyone else went to the remaining local authority schools, some of which had become sink schools. It just so happened that my teaching placement school was one of them. It was underfunded, undersubscribed, only 7 per cent of its students left with five good GCSE grades and, unsurprisingly, it had been judged to be failing. Everything that could break down, had – discipline; staff morale; parent relations – and, just like its vending machines, it regularly failed to deliver. It really was the Wild West – a fact of which I was made painfully aware in the first few minutes of my first day.

As I nervously approached the main school entrance with only a new 100 per cent polyester suit for protection, I was presented with an instant dilemma. My path was blocked by a menacing group of boys wearing hoodies and openly smoking. As I was only moments away from becoming a bona-fide trainee member of staff, I debated whether or not it was my duty to challenge them. I swiftly made the decision that, on this one occasion only, I was prepared to overlook the smoking. You'll understand this had nothing to do with the fact that they were really big and scary looking, but because I was yet to receive my official name badge and lanyard. Anticipating some sort of roughing up, I am embarrassed to say I flinched as they menacingly closed in around me. One lad, whose facial stubble boasted of testosterone levels I had never achieved, demanded to know who I was. Fortunately, once he had established that I was a new trainee teacher, his attitude seemed to soften. He politely introduced himself as Dean McIntyre, a Year Ten student, then informed me that this entrance was currently out of use and directed me to the staff entrance across the way.

Somewhat relieved, I blurted out my thanks and strode off, chastizing myself for so easily falling for negative stereotypes. These were decent kids, for goodness' sake, well-mannered too; why, Dean had even called me 'Sir'. I gave the door he had identified a firm push, and with renewed confidence entered the building . . . only to find I had walked headlong into the boys' toilets. I had the extreme humiliation of having to walk out to the raucous cheers of a triumphant pack of fifteen-year-old boys. I had firmly identified myself to the student body as fair game, even before collecting my name badge and lanyard. Unfortunately, this set the scene for the rest of my placement.

If I'm honest, I really didn't get much teaching done in my placement school. My zoo-keeping skills were woefully inadequate for its clientele, and it took all my effort just to keep them in the room and limit the rioting. However, you would be mistaken for thinking these students were lacking in either motivation or brains. When they put their minds to it, they achieved great things and, in a campaign orchestrated by my new stubbly nemesis Dean McIntyre, they managed to lock me in a cupboard, set fire to the lab, steal my trousers and make me cry. I am proud to say, however, that although I almost lost consciousness when hit on the back of the head by a flying textbook, I did avoid being put into a coma.

I was really hoping Dr Maitland could provide me with some effective behavioural tips on her observation visit. However, things did not go well. A ripple tank, a device full of water used to demonstrate waves, had been left on the front desk. When I tried to move it at the start of my observed lesson, about five litres of water cascaded down my front, triggering a joyous uproar from my students. While Dr Maitland was helping me mop up, the students stole her chair, hid her glasses and flicked ink onto the back of her coat. Clearly rattled by this experience and their ensuing behaviour, where they took turns to tap her on the back and run away, she made an excuse to leave when I was only halfway through the lesson. Sensing another scalp, the class launched into a slow handclap. In a desperate last move, I blocked her exit and pleaded for guidance. What I really needed was some practical advice on how to develop my classroom presence, how to effectively use body language and project my voice, along with some very specific strategies for conflict resolution. Instead of meeting these needs, Dr Maitland mumbled something about boundaries and expectations before scuttling off and leaving me to face my fate alone, clad in damp polyester.

Previously, as a sleep-deprived junior doctor, I had worked at a large district hospital in Liverpool helping to treat patients from some of Britain's most challenged neighbourhoods. Strangely, the anxiety I had experienced back then – trying to cope with the deluge of blood, guts, trauma and death that poured in through the door on a daily basis – was nowhere near as intense as the anxiety I now felt as I struggled to control my classes. The stress generated by a group of teenagers blatantly disobeying you, goading you and, on occasion, laughing in your face is unique, and should really be on the bucket list of adrenaline-seekers everywhere.

These initial struggles with classroom management had me looking like the proverbial rabbit caught in the headlights and triggered a second crisis of faith. I was suddenly consumed with doubts about my suitability as a teacher and wondered whether I had made a terrible mistake in giving up medicine. My medical friends were now not only growing in their clinical confidence but were beginning to reap the material rewards of their labours. They were buying their first new cars, Golfs and Escorts, getting a foot on the property ladder and planning holidays in Tuscany. In contrast, Caroline and I were living in a one-bedroom rented flat in Crystal Palace, were intimately acquainted with the vagaries of London Transport and needed to cap our weekly food spend at £15. It probably wasn't really the best of times to debate throwing in the towel yet again, but I thought I would tentatively broach the subject with Caroline. To give her her due, she did listen very politely to my angst; however, by the end of the conversation I was left in no doubt that there was a real need to get on with it.

JANUARY 1992:
SURVIVAL OF THE FITTEST

My only solace was that none of my tutorial group seemed to have any more control than me, and the only other trainee at my placement school, a mature German student called Manfred, had even less. He was a German chemistry graduate with a PhD in thermodynamics. With impeccable academic qualifications, a sharp suit (100 per cent wool) and natty bow-tie, Manfred had arrived ready to teach. Unfortunately, he was unable to convert the information inside his considerable brain into a format usable by the schoolboys of outer London. I may have struggled, but boy, did Manfred suffer.

One time I was drawn to his classroom by the sound of singing, and looking in, I saw the whole class doing the 'Hokey Cokey' with an extremely agitated Manfred trapped in the middle. I was certain this had not been in the lesson plan he'd shown me earlier that morning. The shenanigans got out of hand and only ended when some of the laboratory door panels were kicked in. Passing his room later in the week, I saw a student crawling into the room through the gap left by the missing panels. I tried to stop him by grabbing his legs and pulling him out. His classmates, spotting his predicament, came to his rescue by grabbing his arms and pulling him in.

After several minutes of puffing and panting on both sides, he managed to wriggle free of me and they finally heaved him in. I burst into the room ready to give them a good dressing-down, but as I could see Manfred happily writing on the board and oblivious to the drama, I decided to leave it. That was until I noticed that the room seemed unusually full, and when a quick headcount revealed forty-two students, I could no longer leave it. It came to light during the subsequent investigation that the class had been trying to see how many extra students they could sneak into Manfred's lesson before he noticed. They had managed an extra twelve before I rumbled them, ten from other classes and two from a neighbouring school.

At the end of the spring term a wary-looking Dr Maitland ventured back into school to give Manfred his assessed lesson observation. Although his lesson was even worse than mine, at least this time she had the courtesy to stay for the duration. Once over, Manfred decided that rather than wait for her in-depth evaluation of his humiliating performance, he would quit. Shouting, *'Nicht mehr'*, he ripped off his bow-tie, threw it on the floor and stormed out of school, never to be seen again. This was a shame, and not because teaching had lost a talent, but because I had quite liked Manfred. Even now, when thermodynamics comes up as a topic of mealtime conversation, I remember him fondly. His departure meant I replaced him at the bottom of the pile and became the go-to target for student misdemeanours great and small.

I used a toy robot named Robbie as a prop to help improve the scientific understanding of my younger classes. Once wound up, he would stagger mechanically down the desk making a loud whirring noise. At the end of a lesson, if the Year Sevens still did not understand something we had covered, I would encourage them to ask Robbie the Robot. I would then answer their questions using my best robot voice. This became a feature of the lesson that the Year Sevens really seemed to enjoy; however, this love for Robbie was not shared by Dean McIntyre and the Year Tens. One lesson, after I had briefly popped out of the classroom to see if I could find an elusive textbook, I returned empty-handed to find that the door had been locked from the inside.

Looking in, I could see the whole class gathered around my front desk with Dean at one end winding Robbie up. He smiled and waved back at me before setting the little automaton firmly on course towards the sink at the other end, within which a beaker of acid had been placed. I banged on the door in vain as they clapped and cheered Robbie on towards his fateful rendezvous with a caustic bath. I could only watch helplessly as, with a final frenzied drum roll, Robbie tottered into the abyss. He never whirred properly again.

Other incidents were more extreme. One afternoon, I was surprised to see one boy's mother turn up to my Year Ten chemistry lesson on the periodic table. Parental support has a very positive effect on learning, so you would have thought her new-found interest in his chemistry lessons would have been welcome. However, she was not visiting to brush up on her knowledge of the noble gases, but rather to sort out another boy who had been disrespecting her in the local community. Completely ignoring me, she asked her son to identify the culprit. It came as no surprise to anyone in the room when he pointed directly at Dean McIntyre. She very calmly extracted a plastic cricket bat from her bag and, without warning, launched herself at him. She repeatedly whacked him with the bat until I eventually managed to get between them and drag her off, but not before I'd received several juicy whacks myself. In the end I needed the help of two teaching assistants and a caretaker to eject her from the site; all the while she hurled a stream of obscenities at me. It left me a bit shocked and a little shaky. There was, however, a silver lining to this unfortunate incident because my attempt to protect Dean seemed to afford me some credit with him. Although he didn't completely abandon his mission to make my life a misery, there was a noticeable reduction in its scope.

When I recounted the incident in the science staffroom, it didn't quite cause the shock and awe I thought it would. I came to the realisation that after years of such antics, the staff were no longer surprised by such outlandish behaviour. At breaktime the whole department would squeeze into the staffroom's two close-set rows of seats, which felt like we were paratroopers awaiting the drop zone. We stayed there, safe and snug, until the bell went, at which point the Head of Science would fling open the door to the corridor. One by one he would pull us to the entrance and shout, 'In the door, ready, jump!' and, clutching our lesson plans, we would leap out into the void. He didn't really do that, but it felt like he should have.

APRIL 1992:
HARD LESSONS

Not everything was as challenging. I was quite enjoying my role as the tutor of a Year Nine form. I was supposed to be supporting their usual tutor, Mr Damerell, but after a couple of days he left me to it. This wasn't a problem, as the tutor group and I seemed to rub along nicely together and the unsophisticated banter of thirty teenage boys came as a welcome relief from the stresses of classroom teaching. Two boys seemed to take a shine to me – Archie Jacobs, or AJ, as he was known, and his best mate David Arnold. AJ, the youngest of seven, was a ragtag of a boy who struggled to fill his oversized hand-me-down uniform. He had an uncared-for look about him, and I knew some concerns had been raised about his home life. Despite this, he was as bright as a button and he and his sidekick David were a right pair of comedians. I watched them in a drama lesson where they performed a hilarious skit on some of the senior staff that had everyone, including the teachers in the room, in stiches. Both boys would linger behind after registration or seek me out at lunchtime and engage me in their entertaining chit-chat. They really were very funny.

As a trainee teacher it took a while to build up my classroom control, although slowly but surely over the coming weeks I managed to develop some rudimentary behavioural techniques – along with a much-needed thicker skin. Not massively thick like a rhino's; more like that of a small lizard, but thicker all the same. Consequently, I began to deliver some stunning lessons, and I mean truly, truly stunning. At least I thought they were, but then I was happily operating in the 'unconsciously incompetent' first stage of teaching. This is where I really didn't know how to teach but was blissfully unaware of this seriously limiting deficiency. It was a rather enjoyable stage to pootle about in, and I embraced the opportunity to be the world's greatest showman.

'How was your lesson?'

'I was great.'

'Did the students learn anything?'

'I was absolutely hilarious.'

'But did the students learn anything?'

'After that masterclass, impossible not to really.'

Subsequent testing indicated otherwise. My top set's test answers clearly demonstrated that they hadn't a clue about anything I thought I'd taught them. They may well have enjoyed my amusing anecdotes and dramatic demonstrations, but they were dazed and confused when it came to the subject matter. They had performed even worse than the third set, and I had the humiliation of having my next two lessons observed by the Head of Science after 'concerns about my teaching' were raised.

I slowly began to twig that teaching is not all about your own performance, and this realisation shifted me uncomfortably into the 'consciously incompetent' stage. Now I was aware that I could not teach very well, and the knowledge that my defective delivery was leading to feeble learning raised my stress levels. I needed to develop the skills that would move me on to the next stage, the 'consciously competent' stage, by refocusing my lessons on student learning rather than them being a showcase for my performing genius. Over the years, experience has shown me that showy raconteurs are not always the best teachers; memorable perhaps, entertaining maybe, at times inspirational, but they are not necessarily the best at getting students to learn. Simply entertaining the troops and being liked is not enough. Good teaching requires many skills: a mastery of the subject matter; creativity; proficient classroom management; and an understanding of metacognition, to name but a few, all of which require time, sometimes many years, to develop.

The majority of teachers spend most of their careers being 'consciously competent'; that is, they know how to teach well, but they still need to think quite hard about it. As this requires a sustained effort, it's one of the reasons why teaching can be so exhausting. However, there are a few enlightened teachers who appear to have escaped the bonds of mortal existence to become 'unconsciously competent'. They inhabit a sort of teaching nirvana where they have gained the ability to deliver excellent lessons without the need for conscious thought. Such Yoda-like figures are held in the highest esteem by other teachers and have the students hanging on their every word.

There was one such superhuman in my department called Miss Hussain, an unassuming middle-aged physics teacher who genuinely appeared to have magical powers. The usually unruly students lined up quietly outside her classroom; they avidly listened when she spoke and were eager to answer her questions. With no visible effort or lesson plan, she seemed to know exactly what to say, how to say it and what to do to get her students to learn. She skilfully managed to get them to do all the hard work, and while they left her lessons shattered with the effort, she rarely broke a sweat.

This was in direct contrast to my lessons, where the simple act of getting my students to take out their pens would cause widespread exhaustion and a cessation of any further activity. Additionally, it was rare for me to finish a lesson without a hoarse voice, large underarm sweat patches and feeling like I had been put through the mill. Annoyingly, Miss Hussain's students also took excessive care of their exercise books, gave their homework in on time and turned up to her lunchtime revision sessions in droves. The briefest flicker of displeasure on her face would be enough to stop most student misdemeanours mid-track. She even had Dean McIntyre eating out of her hand.

Unsurprisingly, her results were consistently outstanding, and she achieved all of this without any of the huffing and puffing of mere mortal teachers. In an attempt to improve my teaching and catch some of her stardust, I invited Miss Hussain to observe one of my lessons. I thought it had gone well, so I was crestfallen when her extensive feedback could best be summed up by a famous quote from the 'real' *Star Wars* Yoda himself: 'Much to learn, you still have, young Padawan . . .'

However, when I acted on her forensic analysis by gathering more feedback on learning throughout the lesson – increasing the pace and the variety of tasks, as well as not talking about myself so much – there was a noticeable improvement in my students' learning. Over the coming weeks, Miss Hussain became a sort of unofficial mentor to me, and I soaked up her advice like a sponge.

There are many different types of teachers, but during my career I have identified five noteworthy teaching personae common to all the schools I have worked in: the Yoda, the Behaviour Beast, the Slopey Shoulders, the Maverick and the People's Champion. Much like the big five safari animals roaming the savannah, these big five teaching beasts can be spotted wandering the classrooms and corridors of schools across the land. Miss Hussain was a prime example of a Yoda, a consistently 'unconsciously competent' teacher; she really did have a gift.

Towards the end of my teaching practice, just when I was beginning to believe I might be able make a half-decent fist of the job, I was rocked by an incident that shook me to the core. I attended the Year Nine options evening, where students, accompanied by their parents, got the opportunity for an in-depth chat with their teachers about their GCSE options. I hovered speculatively around the main hall on the off-chance that any of my tutees needed help with their decisions. Rather unexpectedly this turned out to be a heartening experience, as many of my tutees brought their parents over to discuss their choices with me, and I received several positive comments about my time as their son's tutor. Emboldened by this feedback, I spotted AJ and his parents across the room and decided to go over and introduce myself.

Puffed up with my own sense of self-importance, I said, 'Good evening, Mr and Mrs Jacobs, I would like to introduce myself. My name is Dr Smith, and I am AJ's stand-in tutor.'

Mr Jacobs, a hulking man-mountain, was clearly unimpressed by this revelation, as he simply looked me up and down and said, 'So bloody what?'

Despite being taken aback by this belligerent response and the look of discomfort on AJ's face, I forged on.

'Well, I wondered whether you needed any help with AJ's choices.'

'No need, mate, it's all sorted. He's doing resistant materials, history and business.'

'Oh, right,' I said, somewhat surprised. 'Isn't he going to do drama, then? He has a real talent for it, you know. I saw him in a drama lesson the other day and he was absolutely brilliant.'

Mr Jacobs snapped back immediately, 'Look, matey, you're not listening to me. I've just told you what he's doing, and it don't involve pratting about doing effing drama.'

Applying my formidable intuition to the situation, I

concluded that it was probably best to end the conversation right there.

'Oh well, never mind. If he doesn't do it at GCSE then he could always audition for the school play on Thursday. He's such a star, it would be a real shame to let his talent go to waste. Anyway, it was very nice meeting both of you,' I said, hoping to finish on a placatory note. However, this seemed to infuriate Mr Jacobs even more.

He stepped towards me aggressively and thrust his face so close to mine that I could smell the alcohol on his breath. Then he repeatedly prodded me in the chest as he snarled, 'Listen, short-arse, don't you go putting bloody ideas in his head, alright? Drama is a waste of bloody time. I'm not letting him mess about with a bunch of poofters, so shut your cakehole and get your nose out of our business. Come on, Doreen, let's get out of this dump.'

With that he stormed off with Mrs Jacobs in tow, leaving me temporarily shaken and stunned by the ferocity of his response. An embarrassed AJ tried to apologize for his father's outburst.

'Really sorry about that, Sir, but he's just lost his job. Don't worry though, 'cos I'll go to them auditions on Thursday,' he said, before he hurriedly chased off after his parents. It was an incongruous exchange in an otherwise upbeat evening, but because I was back at university for the next few days, it was soon forgotten among my lectures, tutorials and the obligatory exchange of placement horror stories.

When I returned the next Monday for my last week of teaching practice, AJ was absent from registration and David Arnold didn't know where he was. He helpfully suggested that AJ might have caught a cold, and I later ended up wishing this had been the cause of his absence. At lunchtime the child protection officer called me in to explain the situation.

On the previous Thursday, AJ had attended the auditions as I'd encouraged him to do, but they had overrun, so he was late getting home. Mr Jacobs, who had been drinking all afternoon, was waiting for him. He was furious that AJ had defied him and, in a drunken rage, had beaten him senseless, breaking his jaw and fracturing his skull. AJ was now in hospital and Mr Jacobs had been taken into police custody. I was truly shocked by this appalling turn of events and, despite people telling me I wasn't responsible for Mr Jacobs' actions, I couldn't help thinking that I had been a major contributor by winding him up and encouraging AJ to go to the auditions. My self-important interference had had disastrous consequences.

AJ did not return before I finished my placement, so I rang Mr Damerell several times later that term to find out how he was getting on. He told me that although AJ had recovered well physically, they were worried the attack would have a lasting psychological effect on him.

This was harrowing news and affected me deeply for some time. After lengthy reflection, however, I found it reinforced my desire to teach and to continue to 'put bloody ideas in students' heads'. My hope was that rather than resulting in tragedy, they would spur some of my students on to discover an interest or ignite a passion for their future.

Affirmation for this lofty aim came from a most unexpected source. On the last day of my placement, Dean McIntyre was loitering behind at the end of my final Year Ten lesson. I braced myself for what I thought would be a parting prank, but instead he came over and held out a plastic bag.

'What's this then, Dean?' I asked warily.

'Um, it's a leaving present, Sir,' he said, looking awkward.

'Oh,' I said, completely taken aback. I opened the bag to find it contained a partly used bottle of Calvin Klein aftershave.

'Well, thank you very much, Dean,' I said, 'that really is very kind of you.'

'Well, I know we gave you a hard time, Sir, but actually your lessons were alright. I liked 'em. In fact, I was thinking of doing science next year at college; what do you think?'

I was genuinely flabbergasted.

'I think that's fantastic news, Dean. I'm sure you'll do really well.'

'Really? Sweet. Though I do know I'll need to stop messing the teachers about so much,' he said sheepishly.

'Well, you won't be surprised to hear I agree with you on

that one, Dean. My advice would be to focus on the science.'

I spared him any further discomfort by flipping the conversation round and asking him whether he had any parting advice for me.

'Well, there are two things I would say, Sir,' he said, suddenly looking serious. 'One, is that you need to get yourself a decent suit – that one is way too shiny – and two, never ever let a class smell your fear, 'cos otherwise they'll 'ave ya. Just like we did,' he added with a smile.

It was difficult to argue with such chalk-face gems as these, and it was better practical advice than any I'd received during Dr Maitland's long tutorials, so I thanked Dean and wished him well for the future.

'Nice one, but make sure you don't go telling none of the others about the present, Sir,' he said, still firmly in charge.

'Dean, you have my word,' I replied.

'Wicked. Well, good luck, Sir,' he said, grinning.

He gave me a final nod before sauntering off down the corridor and, as I watched him go, I considered our conversation. It had been a small, seemingly insignificant exchange but one that raised my spirits high; the feeling that I might have made a positive difference to Dean McIntyre's future gave me a buzz similar to the one I'd had as a doctor, helping people get better. It was a heady, potent feeling and I knew I wanted more. It convinced me that finally, not only had I placed my ladder up against the right wall, but I had also stepped up onto the first rung of the journey towards becoming a Hero Head. It felt like I was on my way at last, and surely it would only be a matter of time before I completed the seemingly simple task of scaling the remaining rungs. I was locked, loaded and ready to teach.

Part Two: Newly Qualified

AUTUMN 1992:
REALITY BITES

Thanks largely to the brilliant mentoring of Miss Hussain, I passed my teacher training. The national shortage of science teachers at the time also worked in my favour. I think the need to maintain a steady supply of science and maths teachers meant that the Department of Education had lowered the bar enough for all the trainees to pass our course. Manfred really should have hung on. Buoyed by our success we applied for our first jobs, and I was jammy enough to get a position in one of those well-funded grant-maintained schools I mentioned earlier, while Caroline secured herself a job at an inner-London primary.

I thought it must have been the combination of my excellent observed lesson and incisive interview answers that had got me the job in this comfortable leafy-suburb school, but apparently not. The Head of Science later told me that the Head, who had led the interviews, set great store by a pair of well-polished shoes. Thank goodness, then, that alongside the many hours I had spent preparing for the interview questions, I had set aside five minutes to buff up my Dr Martens. The resultant gleam meant I had ended up in a well-funded school with reasonably well-behaved students.

When the science technician showed me to my new laboratory, full of shiny Formica bench tops and mini sinks, then casually opened a cupboard to reveal row after row of neatly stacked textbooks, I think I actually cooed. There was plenty enough for one textbook per student, the holy grail of my placement school, with the added bonus that they had all been written in the same century in which I was born. To my delight I found that alongside these plentiful resources, my behaviour techniques seemed sufficient to keep most of my new classes in order, so I felt that maybe here things might be a little less demanding than they had been on teaching practice.

If only! By the end of the first term, both Caroline and I were shattered and spent, left reeling by the harsh realisation that teacher training bears no real resemblance to being a full-time teacher. The effort required just to keep our heads above water left us shell-shocked, as we found ourselves caught up in a relentless cycle of lesson preparation, teaching and marking.

Just preparing my lessons was challenge enough. Having a full timetable meant that up to five times a day a fresh wave of animated, overexcited adolescents would burst through the lab door expecting to be taught science in a knowledgeable and engaging way. I never managed to get around to being quite as engaging as I would have liked, because I found I was having to· frantically relearn most of the knowledge. The last time I'd seen much of this science was when I was at school myself, so it was a battle to stay one step ahead of my students. I found that I still knew precious little about plants; I discovered it was not humanly possible to make the nitrogen cycle exciting; and, as for electricity – well, I hadn't really understood it the first time round. If this wasn't bad enough, the students at this school had the audacity to do all the homework I set them. Not only was I expected to mark it, along with any other assignments or tests they had done, but I was also supposed to mark the rest of their classwork as well.

At Christmas, while on leave from frontline hostilities, I took a few minutes to calculate how many individual comments I had written during my first term; my conservative estimate topped twenty thousand. Planning and marking had come to dominate our weeknights and weekends – with a corresponding nosedive in our social life. Anything that threatened the precious time we had earmarked to work caused an instantaneous rise in both tension and blood pressure. Garry, a good friend from medical school, was a persistent threat.

'Hi Nick, we haven't seen you two for a while. Do you and Caroline fancy coming to the comedy club tomorrow night with the rest of us? We've got free tickets to see Frank Skinner.'

'What, on a Wednesday night?'

'Yeah, comedy club, Wednesday night, for an evening of beer and laughter. You still remember beer and laughter, don't you?'

'But it's a school night.'

'And?'

'Well, we can't go out on a Wednesday night, because Wednesday night is a school night.'

'Surely not going out on a school night is something that only applies to small children?'

'The problem is I've got two sets of class books and a test to mark, and I haven't even begun to prepare my sixth form lessons yet.'

'Well, never mind all that. Surely you can wing it. I'll buy you a drink. In fact, I'll buy you several drinks. Come on, Captain Sensible, what's the worst that can happen?'

'What's the worst that can happen? What's the worst that can happen? If my lessons aren't organized properly then the students will start to misbehave. If I don't mark their books, then the parents will write in to complain. If I don't hand back their marked tests then the students won't know what they don't know; and if I don't prep for my sixth form, they'll ask questions I don't know the answers to and I'll lose the small amount of credibility I've worked so bloody hard to earn.'

I realized I was pacing up and down and ranting down the phone. Although I did my best to apologize for my unseemly outburst, the damage had been done and, understandably, over the term, Garry's invitations gradually petered out. I realized that, just like being a junior doctor, explaining how much work you have to do is difficult to appreciate and of very, very limited interest to people outside of your profession. It was far better to find a fellow teacher and moan the socks off them. Conveniently for me, I lived with one, and at the times she wasn't available I could always call Huxley from my tutorial group.

It wasn't even as if all the preparation, teaching and marking was the half of it. In those days the chalk-face was a pretty rough place to be, and the standard tools at our disposal were primitive. Blackboards and chalk, paper registers, overhead projectors and Banda machines (poor-quality manual copiers, beloved for their alcohol fumes) had yet to be replaced by whiteboards and pens, computers, short-throw ceiling projectors and photocopiers. On top of this there was my tutor group to take care of, reports to write, equipment to request, assemblies to listen to and parents' evenings to attend – along with the hundred and one other things required of a full-time teacher.

Over the holidays Caroline and I slowly recovered from our traumatic first term by following a strict regime of comfort food, DVDs and minimal movement, so that by the beginning of January, just as the UK prepared to launch itself headfirst into the new European single market, we prepared to launch ourselves headfirst into a new term.

SPRING AND SUMMER 1993:
LEARNING THE ROPES

I reasoned that if I was going to be a headteacher I would need to develop my public-speaking skills and learn how to deliver high-quality assemblies. Early on this term, in response to the increasing number of students being caught smoking on-site, the opportunity to deliver an assembly on the dangers of smoking presented itself. With my medical background and a sudden rush of blood to the head, I volunteered. I didn't really think the assembly would be a big deal – more like teaching a very large lesson. It was only on the morning of the assembly, as the hall began to fill up with hundreds of students, that I realized it was perhaps a bigger deal than I'd first thought, and I began to feel a little nervous. To my consternation I also noticed that most of the tutors, many of the other teachers and a good selection of support staff had turned up to watch. They were interested to see just what this young upstart with the impertinence to give a whole-school assembly after only his first term was made of; unfortunately, it turned out to be not very much.

As I anxiously scanned through my notes, I was suddenly conscious of my heart hammering in my chest. Then, when

I got to the lectern and looked out to see a thousand pairs of eyes staring right back at me, I developed an instant dry throat and a nervous cough. The result was that my bold opening statement resembled the high-pitched croak of a mating frog and things went pretty much downhill from there. At no point was I in control of proceedings. I had to contend with the continual hum of background chatter interspersed with sporadic giggling, which further shot my nerves and made me lose my thread. Even my hilarious crowd-pleasing jokes misfired. As the students weren't at all interested in my anti-smoking message, I failed to hold their attention and it ended up being a humiliating experience. Although the kinder teachers threw me some encouraging words afterwards, even my own generous assessment rated the assembly somewhere between substandard and abysmal.

It was an early setback to my aspirations but, despite this dent to my ego, I remained undeterred. I really needed to know how to do it better, so I resolved to improve my public-speaking skills by closely observing the experts. Luckily, I had to wait only a week before being given a masterclass in one of the skills required: crowd control.

Mr Freely was one of the deputies at the school, and despite being a mere five foot three inches tall he was the teacher the students most feared. He enjoyed total control over them. When they heard the click of his metal Blakey's (shoe protectors) coming down the corridor, it was like

Moses and the parting of the seas; the students squeezed to the sides desperate not to get in his way. They lowered their eyes to avoid drawing attention to themselves.

Mr Freely took the next assembly and, unlike in mine, the forms entered silently, sat in immaculate rows and listened in silence to his every word. Early on he spotted a Year Eight boy make the fatal error of whispering out of the side of his mouth to his friend. Mr Freely singled him out and made him stand motionless at the front of the hall. It was a really hot day and the sun beat through the windows directly onto him. After about ten minutes the boy, overcome by the heat and lack of blood returning from his legs, fainted and crumpled to the floor. Mr Freely ignored him completely and continued with the assembly. A few members of staff started forward to his aid, but before they got near, Mr Freely roared at them to stay where they were. As cool as a cucumber he kept talking while the boy lay moaning on the floor. It was another five minutes before he finished speaking, and it was only after everyone had been dismissed that he let the staff attend to the poor student, who thankfully made a full recovery.

Aside from the overt lack of humanity, Mr Freely's actions would contravene the majority of our policies nowadays. However, this was back then, and staff were grateful to Mr Freely for re-establishing the 'no talking in assembly' rule that I had done so much to undermine the week before. Although I never quite had the bottle to replicate this type of approach, and consequently never achieved a similar level of control, I did go out and buy a pack of Blakey's so that I too could click down the corridor.

My colleagues and I all benefited from having Mr Freely in our ranks. If we found that a student was starting to play up, the mere threat of some face-to-face time with Mr Freely would result in a rapid restoration of calm and compliance to our classrooms. Although most teachers would agree that we shouldn't really be scaring our students like this, there is an undoubted advantage in having this type of teacher roaming the corridors. Behaviour Beasts like Mr Freely represent the second of my big five teaching types.

During this term I also experienced my first few parents' evenings and made all the classic rookie errors. I talked effusively to a smiling mother about all the excellent things Sally had achieved over the last term, only for her to reply, 'It sounds like Sally is doing just great and, don't get me wrong, I'm really pleased for her, but are you able to tell me anything about my daughter Chloe?'

I overestimated the difference meeting some parents would have on their offspring. One concerned set of Year Nine parents nodded in solemn agreement as I explained the issue of their son's behaviour and they assured me they were going straight home to give him a good talking-to. Next lesson, when his behaviour seemed, if anything, worse, I lost my cool and shouted at him across the class: 'Didn't your parents say anything to you after our meeting last night?'

'Yes, Sir, they told me I was to ignore Dr Smith because he's a complete twat,' came his gleeful reply.

I was desperate to have stern words with the mother of another Year Nine student called Hannah, an absolute demon who did no work and was constantly disruptive. In preparation I had scribbled down the key points I wanted to make; however, her mother stumped me with her opening gambit. Reaching across the table and clasping both my hands in hers, she said, 'Oh, I'm so pleased to meet you, Nick. Can I call you Nick? I'm hoping to hear some good things about Hannah, my little angel. That's what I call her, you know, my little angel, because that's exactly what she is. Every day she makes me feel so proud. Did you know you are her favourite teacher? Now, how is she getting on in biology?' Suffice to say, I don't think I managed to get all my points across.

Parents' evenings present a logistical challenge due to the number of parents who want to be seen in such a short space of time. This creates pressure for teachers to stick tightly to the schedule to avoid putting everyone else out of sync; however, it's easy to get blown off course. Appointments can overrun for a variety of reasons: naturally some parents will talk about their offspring forever if you let them; others have been eagerly waiting for this opportunity to complain about you to your face; but a common reason for overrunning is having appointments with parents who lead challenging lives. Parents' evenings sometimes provide a glimpse into the domestic struggles of your students, and this was true for Maria Fenton, one of my Year Ten students.

Maria was a bright student; she had a first-rate scientific brain and was naturally curious. She was able to assimilate scientific knowledge quickly and apply it to practical situations. However, while she excelled in the classroom, her homework was scrappy, her test scores never reflected her true ability, and I became increasingly frustrated by her failure to convert her classroom promise into hard results. Several times I took her aside at the end of a lesson to challenge her lack of effort with homework and revision. She would avoid my eyes and shuffle uncomfortably while mumbling about not having had the time.

This type of response would have immediately raised questions in teachers more experienced than me but, keen to impress my superiors, I was more concerned about how her underperformance was affecting my class data. I simply told her she had to 'jolly well make the time', and I made sure that she signed up for a parents' evening appointment where I didn't intend to pull any punches. I would tell Maria's parents just how her idleness was letting her down and hopefully this would resolve the offending blip in my data. The meeting turned out to be a sobering experience. The parents' evening was quite noisy because several young children were running around unsupervised and, despite the frequent frowns of staff and parents, whoever was in charge of them was doing a pretty poor job.

When it was time for Maria's appointment, I was fully prepared to dispense some strong words but was immediately thrown off balance when all these unattended children converged on my desk. Out of the throng Maria appeared carrying a youngster on one arm and supporting her mother on the other. Mrs Fenton didn't look well at all and seemed exhausted by the effort to walk across to me; it took her a while to compose herself. She explained that she had contracted pneumonia after the birth of her sixth child and had subsequently developed post-viral fatigue. This meant that even the slightest exertion exhausted her, and she struggled to look after the children. Matters were made worse when her husband, unable to cope with the situation, revealed his lack of backbone by fleeing the nest. As the eldest child, the responsibility for the family had fallen squarely on the shoulders of Maria. It turned out that far from being lazy, Maria spent all her time out of school being her mother's carer and looking after her undisciplined five siblings, who were messing about in front of me. Maria had been too embarrassed to tell anyone at school, and even as her mother was explaining the situation to me, she looked mortified. My God, I thought to myself, what sort of blinkered brute totally lacking in compassion was I? How had I missed the signs of her struggle?

I mentally shredded my script and refocused the meeting on how we could best support the family. I promised to get our pastoral teams to investigate what help was available, and I came up with some strategies we could use in school. I offered Maria the use of my lab at break and lunch if she needed to complete any work and told her I would ask the other staff to be flexible with their deadlines. We could also explore the possibility of her dropping some other subjects, so she could use the gained time to work on her core studies. By the time we had finished our discussion, Maria appeared mightily relieved that her issues were out in the open and that she might get some help. The session had overrun considerably, and although there was some discernible tutting and sighing from the waiting queue, overrunning with parents like Mrs Fenton is entirely justifiable. Parents' evenings can often highlight family issues like these and help us to nurture the positive parent relationships that might help. In the case of Maria, the help we managed to arrange enabled her to become one of our top-performing students in the summer exams.

SUMMER 1993:
GO WEST, YOUNG MAN

By the end of the year, although exhausted, I had improved my teaching a little and gained a general understanding of how schools work. I had come to properly appreciate that students were not standard-sized empty vessels, simply waiting for me to fill them with knowledge, but were a complex group of irregular and often erratic individuals, each with differing backgrounds and needs. Although teaching them could sometimes be a challenge, it could also be an incredibly uplifting experience, and to my delight I found myself enjoying it immensely.

There was no doubt in my mind that I had made the right move, and both Caroline and I remained keen to continue with our teaching careers. Sadly, this is not true of all new teachers, and two-thirds of my tutorial group had already fallen by the wayside. As well as Manfred not making it through his teaching practice, the demands of the first year of teaching also sent the marketing executive back into marketing and forced the two other younger trainees to finally think of something better to do. That left only Huxley and me still in the game. In recent years, around 15 per cent of teachers have left the profession after their first full year, rising to over 30 per cent by the fifth year.

Those leaving cite pay, workload and government policy as key issues, but I believe many are stunned by a full timetable, the complex demands of their students and the realisation that the support they got when they were training is about as good as it gets. Schools have not received the funding necessary to provide the level of support that would prevent some of these new teachers floundering around in the 'consciously incompetent' stage of teaching for longer than is good for them. The attitude seems to be one of sink or swim, and there is an awful lot of sinking going on. This rate of attrition is an enormous waste of time, effort, money and talent and the government needs to mitigate against it. The new Early Career Framework introduced in 2021 is long overdue, and I really hope that this extension of training into the early years of teaching will go some way towards halting the exodus. The key is to fully fund reduced timetables so that fledgling teachers have protected time to train, plan and reflect properly. There is precious little chance to do this during a hectic five-period day.

As to my leadership ambitions back in 1993, apart from my one lame assembly, I hadn't really made any progress, so I was perturbed to hear that Huxley had impressed so much during his first year that his school had offered him a position as Head of Year. It was clear I needed to get my finger out.

I would have liked to have continued teaching in this leafy suburban school, but Caroline and I had both tired of city life and we planned to marry that summer and move back to her hometown in rural Cornwall. So I applied for a job in her old secondary school, while she secured a position in a nearby village primary.

I was under pressure to nail the job at Caroline's old school as it was the only post to have come up in the local area. The only other candidate to consider the position worthy of an application also came from London, but while he had planned to come down early by train on the day of the interview, I had driven down the night before. This turned out to be fortuitous, because due to torrential overnight rain, flooding on the Somerset Levels had rendered the West Country rail line impassable. Unable to make it down to this provincial backwater in time for the interviews, the other candidate withdrew. When Mr Hodin, the Head of Science, told me this news, I made appropriately sympathetic noises about the other candidate's misfortune while inwardly whooping and hollering. Surely as the last man standing, the job was mine. Apparently not.

After a short tour and an observed lesson, Mr Hodin – an academic with an eye for detail – felt it necessary to take me aside for a pep talk before the panel interview. It was clear he had reservations both about my general laxity and my ability to convince the panel of my suitability because he said, 'I need to let you know that you shouldn't assume that just because you're the only candidate, they will automatically give you the job. They may well not appoint, so you might want to sharpen up a bit.'

I realize that 'growth mindset' wasn't a thing in those days, but this really wasn't the endorsement I needed to receive minutes before my interview. I don't know what it was about my image, but it didn't seem to instil confidence in others.

If I had any hopes of becoming a leader, then there was a real need to work on my image, and feeling riled by Mr Hodin's words, I decided to do something about it there and then. Sod them, I thought. I'll show them what I'm made of! Didn't they know I was going to be a headteacher? Fired up, I flounced into the interview and gave the panel both barrels. After deliberating for much longer than I would have liked, they eventually offered me the job. My interpretation of the delay was that with my new-found confidence I had aced the interview and they had taken some time to bask in their good fortune. An alternative explanation was that they had been heatedly debating the option of readvertizing before concluding it was too expensive.

SEPTEMBER 1993:
IN LOCO PARENTIS

Caroline's old school was a rambling comprehensive with a large rural catchment and the students were bussed in from the outlying farms and villages. A significant number of these students intended to leave school at the earliest opportunity to work on the local farms or in related trades and businesses. They were amiable enough if you left them alone, but if you tried to get them to learn about fractional distillation or iambic pentameter they resisted strongly. In fact, if you applied too much pressure they would stay at home and work for their families, some of whom were not the most supportive of parents from a teacher's perspective.

One such family was the Bonners, who ran a mixed

farm on the edge of Bodmin Moor. There were six Bonner boys in total and four of them came to our school. They were a rough-and-ready lot and their attendance at school depended entirely on the needs of the farm. Matthew, the oldest Bonner, would sporadically attend my Year Eleven science class. He was a good-natured lad with a ruddy complexion and huge ham fists, and although he liked doing practical experiments, it would not be unreasonable to say that he sometimes lacked the precision and finesse required. This was highlighted during one of the GCSE chemistry experiments, which involved using thin and fragile glass pipettes. I had very carefully shown the class how to attach the plastic pipette fillers to the long slender tubes. I made it very clear that when they pushed them together, they must hold the pipette right at the top, as close to the filler as possible, because if they held it further down, there was a chance they might snap the tube.

'... and the last thing you want to do is to ram a broken tube into your hand!' I said jokingly.

It was an unfortunate choice of words because, sure enough, five minutes later, the last thing Matthew did was to ram a broken tube into his hand. Despite the stream of blood running down his arm and dripping onto the floor, Matthew seemed completely unfazed.

I could only imagine that such injuries must have been commonplace on his farm because he didn't even blink when I removed a two-centimetre section of glass pipette from his meaty palm with a pair of tweezers. I thought the wound would need a couple of stitches and was worried there might be some glass splinters lodged in his hand, so I arranged to take him to the community hospital and told him I would ring his parents to meet us there.

'Seriously, Sir, it'll be fine, it's just a scratch,' he protested. 'Don't go bothering my dad. He won't want to come all the way into town.'

When I rang his dad, I discovered that Matthew was right, he didn't, and he couldn't understand why I didn't make Matthew walk back home on his own. In the end I had to insist that someone come to collect him. After the X-ray eliminated the presence of any glass, the doctor made quick work of suturing his hand, but we had to wait another two and a half hours before Mr Bonner finally turned up. I was mistakenly expecting at least a smidgeon of gratitude, but it was immediately clear that I had put Mr Bonner out, and I instead found myself being cross-examined as to how I had let his son get injured. Had I followed the correct safety procedures? Could I provide him with a copy of my risk assessment? How long had I been teaching? Did I know what I was doing? He was still complaining loudly when he left and let everyone in the waiting room know he was considering making a formal complaint against me.

As well as being a bit worried about this – I had not been threatened with an official complaint before – I was also outraged. I had taken all the appropriate precautions and, although Matthew was a good lad, it was entirely his fault that he had injured himself. This concern about the standard of health and safety in my lessons was completely ludicrous, as it had only been a short while earlier that I'd had to persuade Mr Bonner not to make his son walk home for miles on dangerous country roads in the dark.

I experienced the dichotomy of acting 'in loco parentis' – it is my legal responsibility to take on some of the functions and responsibilities of a parent while their child is in my care. I don't have any problem with this; parents need to know they are leaving their children in the care of someone who has their child's best interests at heart. What I do find galling is the double standards shown by some parents in holding teachers liable for not delivering levels of care far higher than they ever provide for their kids.

It was common knowledge that the Bonner boys drove tractors on and off the road and operated all manner of dangerous farm machinery. Just weeks earlier I had heard Matthew boasting to his mates that his father had let him borrow his shotgun to shoot rabbits, so the idea that Mr Bonner wanted to see my risk assessment for using a pipette filler was absurd.

The incident further demonstrated to me that the role of a teacher was much more than just looking after a student's academic progress; I was responsible, and unfortunately liable, for much, much more. Luckily, in the end, a complaint never materialized because Matthew turned sixteen the next week, and with the lambing season in full swing, he never returned to school and was set free to operate as much dangerous machinery as he liked.

FEBRUARY 1994:
ATTENTION PLEASE, ATTENTION PLEASE!

Many of the teachers who had taught Caroline were still teaching at the school when I took up the post, and this included the Headteacher, Mr Bevan. He was a likeable, cultured man from a bygone era who would wear his university gown to morning assemblies. I was very grateful to him as he often went out of his way to support me as a new member of staff, although there was one memorable occasion, during bus duty, where his support was not quite as effective as I would have liked.

When the weather was inclement, the students would wait for their buses in the hall. On this occasion, not only was it pouring down but my duty partner (you know who you are) failed to turn up. This meant that I had to keep popping out to the front entrance to find out which bus had arrived and then rush back to the hall to call out its number through a loud-hailer to the waiting students. After the first half-dozen buses, I was hot, sweaty and short of breath. It was taking far longer than usual because instead of queuing in neat lines the students were chatting to their friends in one big heaving mass, making it difficult for students to get out of the hall. I was much relieved when Mr Bevan, who was passing, noticed my difficulty and stopped to lend a hand. Great, I thought, the Headteacher would soon re-establish some order.

Taking the loud-hailer from me, he strode up onto the stage and attempted to get the students to form the orderly bus queues they were supposed to. 'Attention please, attention please, stop talking and get into your correct bus queues,' he called out. However, none of the students moved an inch; they continued chatting to each other. He repeated himself several more times, but even with my back-up there was no discernible effect – they completely ignored both of us. After several minutes of trying, he came down off the stage and apologetically asked me to take over, explaining that he had a sore throat and really needed to get to a meeting.

As I watched him go I was flummoxed about what to do next. If together we couldn't get them into orderly lines, then what on earth was I supposed to do on my own?

By this point, however, I had had enough, so I went for something more drastic. I slammed the exit door shut, turned the loud-hailer up to full and bawled at the students, 'Unless you halfwits get into your bus queues now, you can all bloody well walk home.'

Even in those days it was still relatively rare for teachers to swear at students, so there was a semi-stunned silence before they grudgingly ambled into ragged lines and enabled me to complete my duty without further incident. Now, of course I don't recommend swearing at students, especially not nowadays, when any outburst is likely to be live-streamed, but back then I was young, desperate and there were neither mobiles nor adult witnesses.

I am confident that no teacher has ever uttered the words, 'You know what, I really enjoyed bus duty today.' It is a necessary evil and no reward for a full day's teaching. It usually consists of half an hour trying to control a seething horde of students, some of whom use the time to settle old scores, to snog or to give lip to the duty teachers. It can often become extended, because if anyone misses their bus it is your responsibility to wait around for them to be picked up by their irritated parents. All this performed, of course, while sporting a high-visibility tabard.

In preparation for my impending rise to headship, I had been carefully observing leadership styles in the hope of picking up some useful tips for my future deployment. The Head in my previous school – the one who thought shiny shoes very important – left virtually no footprint around the school, as he rarely ventured out of his office. During my year there, I only ever had two conversations with him and one of those was my interview. On the infrequent occasions that I passed him in the corridor and said hello, he looked both surprised and troubled at my attempt to exchange salutations, and it was clear that he struggled to place me. While I could accept that my sparkling charisma left no discernible trace in his memory, I was perturbed by this lack of interaction.

As time went by, however, I realized that he didn't interact much with anyone else either. During the winter, when there was some coughing and sneezing during one of his rare staff briefings, he told everyone that he no longer caught colds. He claimed that because he had been constantly exposed to different viruses over the years, he had built up an immunity. Although this was medically sound, I think it far more likely that the reason was that, holed up in his office, no one got near him. Despite this reclusive existence, the school still managed to function smoothly, and this was mainly because he had a very personable deputy called Mrs Simmond, who acted as his intermediary.

By contrast Mr Bevan, my current Headteacher, operated by 'managing on the move'. He was forever in and out of classrooms and engaging staff in lively conversations. He would often stop for a chat, interested to find out how I was getting on and to ask how Caroline was doing, and his school footprint was extensive. Although he was no Behaviour Beast, this did not seem to affect the overall effectiveness of the school because his deputy, a fierce PE teacher, was an even bigger Behaviour Beast than Mr Freely.

The key message I gleaned from these early leadership observations was that it was very important to appoint a deputy who could make up for any of the leadership qualities that I lacked. On further reflection, I decided it might be best for me to appoint several, just to be on the safe side.

JANUARY 1995:
THE PERKS OF THE JOB

Just as I was beginning to feel settled at the school, I had my head turned by a dream job at a nearby further education college, where they required a full-time teacher of A-level Biology.

I was surprised I got the job, because I experienced a few car issues on the day of the interview. I had a very old Alfa Romeo Alfasud, which sounds like it should be classy, but was in fact rubbish. The electrics didn't work, it overheated and the windscreen leaked. After many unsuccessful hours trying to find the leak causing the puddle in the driver's footwell, in a fit of frustration I smashed a hole through the floor to get it to drain away. This meant that although I could see the road passing below while driving, my feet did not get wet. Now that I was aware of the importance of shoes in the interview process, I wanted to arrive with mine shiny and dry.

True to form, the Alfasud let me down on the day of the interview. It was pouring with rain, and halfway through the journey the driver's windscreen wiper suddenly flew off into a hedge. Despite my best efforts poking around in the greenery and walking up and down the verge, I couldn't find it. Both my suit (I had now progressed to a wool blend) and my shoes got disastrously sodden in the process. I had to complete the rest of the journey leaning over to look out of the windscreen on the passenger side, a method of driving I would not recommend even to my enemies.

After several near-fatal accidents and a cricked neck, I arrived for my interview shivering and wet. Unfortunately, things got even worse when I went to sit in the car at lunchtime to collect my thoughts. I was convinced I had parked at the top of the steep car park, but the Alfasud was nowhere to be seen. Scratching my head and scanning around, I finally spotted it right at the very bottom of the car park. It was rammed into a smart Mercedes; the owner of which I presumed was the cross-looking lady standing next to it. I learnt two things when I walked down to face the music: one was that the handbrake had been loose, and two, that this very cross lady was the vice-principal about to interview me for the job. I can only conclude that the other candidates weren't up to much because even though I needed to exchange insurance details with her, she gave me the job and triggered one of the most enjoyable spells of my teaching career.

I found life as a lecturer in an FE college very different to that of a teacher in a school. The college had thousands of students doing hundreds of different courses across multiple sites. All the students were over sixteen, many were adults, many were part-time and, crucially, none of them were obliged to be there; they had all chosen to take these courses. Consequently, the atmosphere was very much more relaxed, and it only took a short while for me to get used to the lack of uniform and to being called Nick by my students.

Most of the courses at the college were vocational, and this provided staff with several perks. I could get the Alfasud serviced for free by the students on the vehicle maintenance course. While they were working on the car, I could treat myself to a haircut from the students doing hair and beauty and then round things off with a three-course meal with silver service, courtesy of the catering students. It's true there was a degree of risk involved in all of these – they were learning after all – but what was the worst that could happen? Well, I could develop diarrhoea and vomiting or have my brakes fail on the way home and, most frightening of all, end up with a mullet, but on balance I felt these were risks worth taking.

There were considerably fewer pastoral expectations placed upon me as a lecturer than there had been when I was a teacher because students with non-academic problems went straight to student services, a hub of specialized staff specifically employed to support their pastoral needs. Consequently, with no tutor group to register, no assemblies or school events to attend, no tutorials to deliver and no behavioural issues to speak of, I was able to embrace the opportunity to focus solely on my teaching. It helped enormously that the two other biology lecturers, Dr Court and Dr Yates, not only generously shared their wealth of knowledge and expertise, but also gifted me a wonderful timetable.

I taught four groups the same section of the A-level Biology syllabus, meaning that by the time I taught the same lesson for the fourth time, I had been able to trial and evaluate it, iron out any issues and upgrade the resources so that I had crafted a thing of beauty. In schools it might be a year or more before you got to teach the same lesson again, and often it's only then that you suddenly remember the worksheet you're using is unclear, or that the demonstration doesn't work very well. This set-up really could not have been better, so it was not surprising that during my time at the college I felt my A-level teaching come on in leaps and bounds. The downside to all this was the marking. Setting just one homework assignment a week could generate over a hundred essays, maybe three hundred pages of A-level marking, and of course we set more than one task a week and tested them regularly as well. This onerous load was partly compensated for by the structure of the college day, which finished around 5 p.m.

Although this was much later than in schools, it meant that we had a glorious hour and a half for lunch. It is difficult to overestimate the difference this substantial break in the day had on our wellbeing. In schools I had been used to short, manic lunchtimes involving rushed meetings, constant interruptions and frantic last-minute planning. Lunch often consisted of a few snatched mouthfuls while hurrying down the corridor towards afternoon lessons. Not so at the college, where there was oodles of time for all manner of things, including getting some of that marking out of the way. I chose to make the most of the time by running to the beach every day with a group of like-minded staff. There was plenty enough time to get back, get showered and enjoy a relaxed lunch at one of the college's numerous food outlets. One blisteringly hot lunchtime in summer, we ran to a beach where a stream plunged over the cliff edge, forming a small waterfall that fell onto rocks. Hot and sweaty, we took turns to receive a full-body shower by standing underneath its refreshing cascade. As I looked out at clear blue skies and a shimmering sea, I wondered whether teaching could get any better.

The only fly in the ointment was that my quest to become a leader had stalled, or, more accurately, hadn't even got started. Luckily this changed at the start of my second year, when I finally got the chance to try my hand at some management, albeit mainly administration. They needed someone to coordinate a new sports studies course they were creating, and I seized the opportunity to take this small step up on my career ladder. It involved co-ordinating the delivery of various elements of the course by lecturers from different faculties, collating all the student grades and managing the coursework. Admittedly it was unpaid, and I was not actually in charge of anyone, but not only did it do wonders for my self-esteem but, joy of joys, I was able to turn the pokey little back room they had given me to store the coursework into an office. From that point onwards, I took the liberty of referring to myself as 'Head of Sports Studies', and in conversation I brought up the fact that I had an office as often as possible.

In her haunting masterpiece, 'Chinese Café/Unchained Melody', Joni Mitchell repeatedly reminds us that nothing lasts for long. This wistful lament to the passing of time was unfortunately also true of my time in further education. After three highly enjoyable years, financial pressures led to the teaching staff on the Senior Leadership Team being replaced by business types. The college turned much more corporate and much less personal. 'Bums on seats' became more of a priority than the quality of delivery. The vocational perks and advantageous teaching set-up were no longer enough to keep me. Although I was still the self-proclaimed Head of Sports Studies, it was a title that did little more than satisfy my vanity. I led and managed no one, and the flat management structure at the college meant there were few opportunities for me to progress. In light of all this, and the inexplicable but significant fact that the pay of a lecturer in further education lagged way behind that of a teacher, I attempted to get back into schools. I applied to be the Head of Biology in another rural comprehensive.

Part Three: Climbing the Greasy Pole

JUNE 1998:

WHAT WAS THE LAST BOOK YOU READ?

I managed to play an absolute blinder on the day of the interview. Having checked several times that my shoes were shiny, both windscreen wipers were firmly attached and my handbrake worked, I arrived at the school without incident. Sadly, I found I was up against five other candidates, all of whom seemed to know what they were talking about and, as the day progressed, I began to wonder if I had overestimated my ability. However, Lady Luck threw me a line. While waiting outside the interview room, I discovered that if I strained my hearing, I could just about decipher the questions the panel were asking. The incumbent interviewee, and current front runner, was being given a hard time.

The Head, who had previously mentioned that she taught history, asked him to tell her about the last book he had read.

Caught off-guard and seemingly flustered by a non-biological question, he struggled to answer before shamefacedly declaring that it had been a football fanzine. The following pregnant silence indicated that this was not the highbrow answer they were seeking. The Head's follow-up question was to ask him to describe something he was passionate about, to which I think he said 'badminton'. This appeared to be unacceptable, as it triggered a near-immediate termination of the interview. The candidate came out looking dazed, knowing that the job might have just slipped through his fingers.

Forewarned, cogs whizzing in my brain, I went in. After the standard job-related questions, sure enough, the Head asked, 'So, Doctor Smith, can you tell us about the last book you read?'

'Why yes, I can. It's a brilliant historical novel called *The Persian Boy* by Mary Renault; have you read it? It's based around the life of Alexander the Great, a figure from the past I have always been fascinated by.'

The Head beamed back at me.

'Why yes, yes, I *have* read it. It's a wonderful book – such feeling, such passion, an absolute epic and a particular favourite of mine. Good, good. Now, perhaps you can also tell us something you are passionate about?'

I described how I loved the outdoors and liked to get up early to walk to the top of one of the local tors. 'Nothing beats looking out across the Cornish countryside in the still morning air,' I said, adding some flavour.

The Head was nodding so vigorously I was genuinely concerned that she might damage herself. I realized I had inadvertently hit the jackpot when she went on to explain that the view from the top of that very tor had been her late husband's favourite. I made a mental note to buy a lottery ticket on the way home.

SEPTEMBER 1998:
RAISED EYEBROWS

I anticipated things would be very different now I was a head of department. It was my first paid management position, and there would be a need for me to behave in a more mature manner, to become more professional, more authoritative. There was a need to purchase cardigans with suede arm patches, corduroy trousers, and ditch the Dr Martens for brogues.

I was looking forward to constructing meeting agendas, to manipulating data to show the department in its best light, but most of all to lead my team onwards and upwards. It was unfortunate, therefore, that the biology department consisted of just myself and the previous Head of Biology, Miss Dobrowska, whose all-round brilliance had led to her promotion as my new Head of Science. Given that she was my direct line-manager and had superior organisational, intellectual and teaching skills, no managing was required whatsoever. In fact, it was impossible for me to deviate in any way from the successful operation she had spent many years putting in place.

She communicated her disapproval of any of my suggested changes through an overly expressive left eyebrow. For example, I would tentatively propose a small change such as, 'So, I was thinking that maybe we should rearrange the order in which we teach the GCSE modules.'

Her left eyebrow would twitch into life and rise to a half-mast position that was code for: 'As a recently conceived management embryo, are you seriously suggesting changes to my long-established and highly successful order?'

Eyes locked on her eyebrow, I would take a deep breath and soldier on: 'Because I thought that maybe if we did the bioenergetics module earlier it might mean the students would better understand the later modules?'

Her left eyebrow would then fully snap to attention, code for: 'So, you actually want to break something that isn't broken? Are you on some sort of medication or are you simply an imbecile?'

A fully raised eyebrow like this was an emergency situation and required urgent action. I would have to save the situation by quickly mumbling something like, 'But having carefully thought it through, I can now clearly see why you organized it as you have and, if it's okay with you, I would like you to keep with the same order as before?'

Appeased, her eyebrow would return to its resting

position and with that, tensions would ease but my latest initiative would be snuffed out. It made me realize that there was more to management than meets the eye (or in this case, eyebrow) and I did not yet have the leadership skills needed to influence my superior. In an attempt to remedy this, I read an article by Daniel Goleman, the well-known psychologist, about the six leadership styles that successful leaders utilize. I carefully considered each in turn to decide which style it would be best to adopt with Miss Dobrowska.

The Coercive 'do what I tell you' and the Authoritative 'come with me' styles were absolute non-starters, as I was too scared of her to try either. The Affiliative 'people come first', the Democratic 'what do you think?' and the Coaching 'try this' approaches also cut no ice, as they were all too touchy-feely for the likes of Miss Dobrowska. This left me only with the Pacesetting 'do as I do' style, but as she had clearly indicated she wasn't willing to do as I did, this was also problematic. In the end, I decided I would teach the modules in my preferred order, and hope that if my class results turned out better than hers, then she might be persuaded to do as I did. Unfortunately, despite me successfully managing the Herculean task of bettering her results, she still wouldn't play ball. Although this unofficial competition between us helped produce department results that were the best in the school, I had still failed to gain any control over the one person I managed (who also managed me), and consequently my leadership development spluttered to a halt. However Miss Dobrowska was a first-class teacher and working closely with and against her meant I gradually improved my teaching further.

The next two years were very pleasant indeed. I was teaching a subject I loved in a good school and Caroline had secured a job in our local primary school. We bought a homely cottage in a small village and went about the business of rearing two children. I could have lived like this forever, and probably would have if my headship ambitions had not been given a much-needed turbo-boost. Just as the millennium turned, and the much-heralded millennium bug crisis failed to materialize, I received the kick in the pants I required. It happened in Conference Room Four of a large seaside hotel in Falmouth while I was on a training course.

JANUARY 2000:
TRAINING: NO PAIN, NO GAIN

Despite the dawning of the new millennium, these were still low-tech times; it was only this year that the humble USB flash drive was invented. There weren't yet any online courses or webinars, so staff development was provided mainly by face-to-face in-service training (INSET). This was usually delivered at school when the pupils were absent or by participation in external courses, and during the autumn term, both of these training methods featured in my development.

Firstly, the Head asked for volunteers to train as facilitators for a self-esteem course he wanted us to deliver. As a science teacher, my impression was that most of this raising self-esteem stuff was a mixture of pseudoscience and psychobabble. However, because it was a three-day residential course in a hotel by the sea, I charitably put my scepticism aside and volunteered.

The course kicked off with the inevitable ice-breaker activity designed to get everyone acquainted with each other. The use of such ice-breakers assumes that the adult professionals assembled do not have the social skills to interact with their course colleagues naturally. In order to forge the lifelong friendships required, it is essential to take part in some sort of 'starter activity'. Such activities should be trivial, embarrassing and, where possible, involve the invasion of personal space, so that they quickly magnify any low-level feelings of awkwardness into ones of deep mortification and shame. On the plus side, there's a wonderful array of exquisitely cringeworthy games to choose from. Over the years I have been made to imitate farmyard animals, make and wear a silly paper hat, and once, as part of a physical task, I ended up with my head in the damp armpit of a stranger less than fifteen minutes after being introduced.

On another particularly memorable course, I was asked to explain that if, instead of being a human, I was a biscuit, what type of biscuit would I be and why. I went for a Jammy Dodger – you know, hard on the outside but soft and gooey in the middle. However, completely against the spirit of the game, a work colleague challenged my choice. He claimed that in addition to my being hard on the outside, I was hard on the inside as well, so I was in fact more of a Rich Tea. The ensuing impassioned argument over my suitability as a Jammy Dodger cast an atmosphere of hostility and resentment over the whole course.

The ice-breaker on this course was called the 'I like me because . . .' game. It required us to pair up and take turns talking at each other for at least three minutes. I think I dried up in under twenty seconds and, despite my partner giving encouraging nods and smiles, the rest of my three minutes passed in silent discomfort. I think I may have even cried at one point. Having witnessed this torture, you would have thought my partner might moderate his response. Not so. Three minutes was barely enough time for him to explain why he was so awesome, and his droning self-praise lasted well into the coffee break. Personally, I think he had too much self-esteem and should have been sent home in disgrace.

Luckily, the ice-breaker did not reflect the excellence of the rest of the course, the content of which hit me like a hammer blow. Without being overdramatic, it was definitely a 'Road to Damascus' experience. The course facilitator was an avuncular Cornishman called Paul Bourdeaux, an ex-primary head who charmed and mesmerized me in equal measure. I was particularly taken with his outlook on leadership and subsequently went on to benefit from his wisdom and mentoring for many years. Paul explored with us how we act in accordance with what we believe, and that we can change our lives by changing the way we think in a deliberate and structured way. It took a well-organized three-day course, peppered with real-life examples and Paul's outstanding facilitation, for us to genuinely believe in this. Yes, I know it still sounds like a load of pseudoscience and psychobabble, but it was compelling, and I got infected. The course encouraged us take a fresh look at what was possible in our lives, and this changed several of us forever.

One participant, a senior leader, handed in a letter of retirement the following week; another left to set up an outdoor activity centre abroad, and one lady rather dramatically left her husband of over twenty years. As for me, after having got myself stranded in the managerial slow lane, I had my headship ambitions reawakened. After three days in the cocoon of Conference Room Four, I emerged transformed, ready to renew my quest. The only problem was that I still had virtually no credible leadership and management experience and, under Miss Dobrowska, that was unlikely to change. Therefore, using the principles promoted by the course, I set about developing the required set of skills.

As soon as I got back to school, I resurrected my mission by putting myself forward to lead a new cross-curricular initiative. As the millennium passed, the government had yet again decided to change the curriculum by introducing a reformed sixth form programme called Curriculum 2000. My role was to implement the 'key skills' of communication, application of number and information technology as part of this. Introducing a new initiative seemed straightforward enough to me – I just needed to bag myself some INSET time to launch it.

For school leaders, INSET is vital because it gives them the opportunity to introduce new initiatives, to roll out government directives and to give staff vital updates on policies that many never knew existed, let alone had read. However, most teachers would rather pass a kidney stone (excruciatingly painful) than endure these sessions because they regard much of it as a waste of their time. They want to focus on their teaching and would prefer to use the time to plan lessons, finish marking, prepare resources and catch up with colleagues in a student-free environment. It is a testament to their professionalism that despite wanting to be elsewhere, most of them manage to sit through such training in a compliant and dignified manner. It was against this backdrop that I prepared to present the key skills to the staff during a twilight INSET session.

As the last presenter of the evening, I became increasingly nervous as my slot approached. The other two presenters were both self-assured, confident in their grasp of the subject matter and their ability to work the audience, and although I was now much more confident speaking to large groups of students, this would be the first time that I had directly addressed my peers. I was conscious of the fact that, based on my performance, judgements would be made about my leadership potential, particularly by those in the hierarchy who held the keys to my advancement. In preparation, Caroline and I had gone shopping to select a shirt-tie combination that most projected the image of someone going places. Even though I felt the blue pinstripe shirt and contrasting bright red tie we had settled on radiated confidence, it didn't stop my stomach from doing somersaults when the Head called me up to the front; I was desperate to make a good impression.

I don't know why I worried really because, quite frankly, it went horribly well. My presentation was dazzling, my overhead transparencies exceptional, and my delivery would have put Winston Churchill to shame – sound familiar? I put the lack of staff questions down to my overwhelming clarity and was quietly confident I had every member of staff on board. There was no doubt in my mind that I had absolutely delivered. However, it soon became painfully apparent that I had delivered diddly-squat. To my horror, my initial evaluation revealed that staff were not enthusiastically promoting the key skills. In some cases, they couldn't even name them. They certainly were not following my plan, and neither were the students – only a handful of whom had filled out any of my lovingly created forms. The low point of my ill-fated approach was when I fretfully challenged one teacher about their lack of engagement, and we ended up shouting at each other down the corridor. I still turn a little red when I think about it now.

Many initiatives later, I can clearly see how I got things so wrong. I had failed to engage the two main groups vital to the success of any school initiative: the Cultural Architects and the INSET Saboteurs.

The Cultural Architects are the staff members the others look up to: the influential heads of department, the 'unconsciously competent' classroom practitioners and the key staffroom players. Without their support your initiative is likely to be dead in the water before you even step up to the podium. In my naivety, I had not attempted to gain the blessing of any of them. In truth, I was not even sure who they were.

Secondly, there is a small core of staff who are less than compliant during INSET sessions and will do all they can to covertly disrupt training. They are known as the INSET Saboteurs and are mostly, but not exclusively, old hands. They've seen it all before and done it all before, and rather inconveniently they are keen to tell everyone that it didn't work then, and it won't work now. They will huddle together, chuntering away among themselves, and occasionally burst into raucous laugher. When you are presenting, this is very disconcerting because you can only conclude, correctly, that they are laughing at you. They are last to their seats and first to the coffee, they can put a big downer on any group work, and, as for ice-breaker activities, well, you can forget it. The INSET Saboteurs need careful handling if they are not to derail your plans, but because I was so focused on my own performance, I must have missed all the frowning, the crossed arms, the loud exhaling and the outbreaks of raucous laughter. It is possible that I even missed some slow handclaps.

I should have chosen more favourable launch conditions as well. The lack of staff engagement was probably compounded by the fatigue that follows a long day of teaching. Just when staff were wondering whether the leftover lasagne would make do for supper, or which child they were picking up from where, I had cheerfully announced extra work. I would have had a much better chance of success if my presentation had been the first item on an INSET morning preceded by unlimited supplies of coffee and Danish pastries.

Suffice to say, the 'key skills' did not turn out to be a great success, either in our school or nationally. It wasn't long before they found their way into the crowded graveyard of government initiatives, but at least in the process I had learnt some valuable early lessons in leadership.

JUNE 2001:
URGENT, BUT NOT IMPORTANT

Despite my ill-fated key skills project, my efforts must have revealed a small glimmer of leadership potential as I was promoted to Deputy Head of Sixth Form. This was very exciting and another crucial step up on my ladder towards headship.

Having realized there was more to leadership than first meets the eye, I began reading books on the subject (in private obviously). I was particularly taken by a time-management matrix known as 'Covey's Squares' – Covey being Stephen Covey, the author of the key motivational book, *The 7 Habits of Highly Effective People*. This is where you have to make judgements about the importance and urgency of various tasks. I retrospectively applied the matrix to my typical week, only to discover that I spent all my time in two of the less effective boxes. My 'urgent' and 'important' box was nearly always full – asbestos in the common room, A-level coursework gone missing, that sort of thing – and if ever there was a lull, I would choose a task from the 'not urgent, not important' box.

This box was filled with things that made no positive difference to my students at all and included tasks such as hanging up a poster of the iconic biodomes that had just been erected down the road at the Eden Project, or rearranging the chairs in the common room so they were symmetrical. I regarded these stress-free tasks as a reward for sorting out all the urgent and important stuff. I did this up until the very end of my teaching career; in my final term as Head, I spent a good twenty minutes discussing a carrot-growing competition while happily ignoring the many more important tasks likely to move the school forward. Back then, though, I discovered that unless I rigorously triaged my in-tray, it was surprisingly easy to let urgent tasks get in the way of the more important ones.

I learnt this the hard way one Friday before half-term, when, to my enduring regret, I let one of my students down. Michelle Foster was one of my Year Ten tutees who had become a troublesome truck. She struggled with much of the academic work and, to avoid embarrassment, she had taken the classic 'if I let everyone think I don't care, then it doesn't matter if I fail' approach. This stance meant she was very disruptive in lessons, argued with her teachers and was forever being sent to see the Head of Year.

As she could be incredibly rude when challenged, she garnered few fans among the teaching staff, but as her tutor I got to see a side to her that they didn't. Despite her couldn't-care-less bravado, she could be kind, and was fiercely protective of the underdog. She once fearlessly stood up to a bunch of older boys who had been shoving a rather timid boy in her class every time they passed him in the corridor. She charged across the corridor and gave the largest of them an almighty shove so that he ended up clattering into the wall.

Although he had clearly hurt his arm, he tried to make light of it in front of his friends, but he was further humiliated when Michelle followed up with a colourful tongue-lashing. Unsurprisingly they didn't do it again.

Another time she forced everyone in the form, me included, to sign a card she had bought for one of the less popular members of the form who had been admitted to hospital for appendicitis. She loved animals, and once rescued a tortoise that had mistakenly wandered onto the playing field and had attracted the unwelcome attention of some Year Sevens. Michelle's mother had told me that she spent virtually all her time outside of school at the local animal rescue centre, working as a volunteer, and by all accounts was highly thought of.

However, over the year her confrontational behaviour escalated, and after several temporary exclusions, she was on the brink of permanent exclusion for persistent disobedience. There was a review meeting being held after school that Friday to decide her fate, and the staff who taught her were given an open invitation to attend. Although she was not supposed to be on-site, I found a very agitated Michelle waiting for me in the car park when I arrived on the morning of her review. She was very worried she would be given her marching orders and pleaded with me to put in a good word for her. It was clear that she really did not want to leave, so I assured her I would attend the meeting and argue her case.

This request belonged in Covey's 'urgent and important' box, and it should clearly have been the priority of my day. However, I let myself get waylaid by other urgent but less important tasks. Alongside teaching four lessons, a field trip meeting at break, and running the junior science club at lunchtime, I was also being pressed by Miss Dobrowska for my analysis of the biology results. It was not rocket science, but it was a very time-consuming task, and I had already missed her deadline by over a week. At lunchtime she let me know in no uncertain terms that as she wanted to work on the data over the half-term, she needed it before I left that evening.

I didn't have any free time until the last lesson of the day, so I found myself under pressure to complete it and, immersed in the task, I lost track of time. Just as I triumphantly handed over my completed data to Miss Dobrowska, I caught sight of the classroom clock and suddenly remembered Michelle's exclusion meeting. In a panic, I sprinted off to the Head's office, only to find, to my dismay, that I was too late; I had missed it. The only person still around was the Head's PA, who rather dismissively told me that as no one had had a good word to say about Michelle, the panel had decided to permanently exclude her.

I couldn't believe that I had let some petty number-crunching override the chance to champion the cause of a troubled student. I don't know whether I would have been able to turn the tide in her favour – after all she had been very difficult and had already been given plenty of chances to sort herself out – but the least she deserved was to have someone fighting her corner. As I had promised her that that would be me, I felt I had really let her down. I passed her and her mother in the street a few weeks later and attempted to talk to them, but they ignored me completely and kept walking. I don't blame them really. The only solace came when I later heard that Michelle had found a permanent job at the rescue centre, which went a little way towards easing my conscience. From then on, I resolved to pay much closer attention to the prioritizing of my in-tray.

Over the years, I have come to realize that one of the secrets of leadership is to spend as much time as possible in the 'non-urgent important' box, as it is here that you can give proper time and attention to the tasks that really make a difference.

SEPTEMBER 11TH, 2001:
9/11

The nine science laboratories were arranged around a large prep room. At one end of the prep room was an assortment of chairs and a coffee table extravagantly referred to as the science staffroom. The staff were in and out of this room all day, and it was lorded over by Hilary, our head technician. As every science teacher knows, the head technician is by far the most powerful person in the department; because the teachers will normally need to interact with them several times a day, it is they who set the tone and culture of the department. A department unfortunate enough to have the type of head technician who, like a dementor from a *Harry Potter* film, sucks the hope and life out of all who enter their domain is in trouble. Just one negative interaction with each of our nine science staff per day would equate to 1,710 negative conversations over a year. No amount of management investment in morale-raising biscuits, duvet days or team building sessions will counteract this type of persistent drip-feed.

You need positive people in positions such as these. Luckily for us Hilary set a lively, upbeat tone for the department, which resulted in a prep room filled with noisy good-humoured banter. Hilary was capable, widely read and by her own admission loved to chat. Her portfolio of gossip was wide-ranging and included discussing the finer details of staff health issues, her opinion on what lesson observation grades each of us would receive from Ofsted, and a running commentary on the health and safety disasters just waiting to happen. It was entirely fitting, therefore, that it was Hilary who announced the 9/11 attacks that month – although the truth was, I almost missed it amid her stream of chatter:

'Yes, so depending on the results of John's blood test we may be needing a new chemistry teacher . . . I forgot to tell you, I couldn't make the agar plates for your practical next lesson because the autoclave has broken down . . . They say they may have to close the school due to Legionnaires in the air-conditioning . . . two airplanes have crashed into the Twin Towers . . . They are going to take us to court to recover the £200,000 they say we owe them . . .' etc.

'Well, Hilary, that truly is a lot of disappointing news,' I replied, 'but can you just run through that bit about the Twin Towers again?'

We were due to have a twilight INSET session after school that day, but when I arrived early, I found the staff already gathering around a TV screen at one end of the hall to watch the news coverage. As soon as the Head got a sense of what was happening, he cancelled the training, but nobody moved as we stayed to watch in horror as the story unfolded. Whispering in hushed tones, we were shocked by the enormity of the event. Eventually, subdued, people drifted off to continue following the story from home.

The next morning my tutor group was very agitated. For many of them it was the first time they had the sense that they were part of something bigger than themselves, and that beyond their lives in this sleepy little market town, all was not well with the world. They had never expressed any interest in world affairs before, but now they wanted an explanation as to why such a thing had happened. I could never have imagined the day before that my tutees would be demanding I give them a summary of Middle Eastern politics during registration. Despite the gaps in my own knowledge, I gave it my best shot and they were the most serious and engaged I have ever seen them. The discussion lasted well into their first lesson.

MARCH 2002:
READY FOR INSPECTION

Early in the spring term the Head received a phone call from the Grim Reaper – the Ofsted inspectors were coming to visit and would require an office, a coffee machine, an unfeasible amount of data and our souls.

As an Ofsted virgin, it was grimly fascinating to watch the inspection process unfold. The Ofsted phone call can be likened to a surgeon telling you there is absolutely nothing to worry about, but they need to open you up for an exploratory look at your insides. Both these scenarios generate a high state of anxiety, and the six-week build-up to the visit, much like the wait for an exploratory operation, was an excruciating time. All normal life ceased as the school became obsessed with the upcoming inspection. Teachers started getting into school earlier and leaving later; books that had remained unmarked all term were suddenly full of helpful red writing. Grumpy old-timers would sidle up to newly qualified teachers and show an uncharacteristic interest in their lesson plans. Meetings were held, briefings were arranged, and the harassed data team felled a forest in order to satiate the demand for stats and facts. There was an awful lot of whispering in corridors. Who was the weak link? Which policies had not been followed? Where were we lacking evidence? There was only one person who welcomed Ofsted with open arms and that was Hilary. She would finally get to find out if her predicted lesson observation grades were accurate.

These were the grades that teachers received from the inspectors who observed their lessons and they were the overriding concern of teachers during an Ofsted visit. Their lessons could be judged to be either: 1) excellent, 2) good, 3) satisfactory, or 4) inadequate, and these grades could make or break newbies and experienced teachers alike. It was therefore unsurprising that during inspection week, staff would desperately try to anticipate which of their lessons would be observed. Please, please let it be my lovely Year Eights and, for the love of God, not my Year Elevens, last lesson after PE, when they arrive half-dressed, hot and sweaty, blood pumping, and it takes at least half the lesson to settle them down. The news of the grades awarded would spread around the school like wildfire, helpfully fanned by Hilary. Can you believe Miss Brown (the Head's favourite) only got a satisfactory? How on earth did Mr Mitchell get an excellent, when most days he can't even remember to put his socks on? Staff receiving excellent or good grades would feign embarrassment and put it all down to luck. Those that received satisfactory or inadequate grades would sob for weeks and explain to anyone who was interested (no one) that this was very unfair because the inspector wasn't a subject specialist, or the class deliberately sabotaged the lesson, etc. I received an excellent for my biology lesson. I really don't know how (my lovely Year Eights) . . . I was so lucky. However, I received a satisfactory for my physics lesson, but this wasn't really fair. Let me explain why. The inspector was a chemistry specialist; however, it was a physics lesson, and it was my difficult Year Elevens, last period after they had all arrived late from PE . . .

Overall, the school was judged to be 'a good school (2) with outstanding features', which was regarded as a favourable result by everyone. Although I was pleased to have survived my first Ofsted, I was genuinely puzzled how this all-important do-or-die encounter brought about school improvement. The hundreds of hours we spent generating all our evidence could have been better spent improving teaching and learning.

After casually pointing out to us the areas they felt we needed to develop, the inspectors had hotfooted it without leaving us any specific clues as to how to improve. To return to my surgical analogy – if a surgeon had opened you up and found an unwanted growth, you wouldn't expect them to sew you back up and tell you they would return in a couple of years to see how you were getting on.

Two decades on and five Ofsted inspections later, the inspection format has changed somewhat, but not for the better. It is clear in my mind that the Ofsted inspection regime is unfit for purpose. In fact, I believe it does more harm than good and has become a monstrosity that dominates the waking thoughts and darkest dreams of headteachers across the country. They must channel an excessive amount of time and energy into being permanently ready for the dreaded phone call that gives just a day's notice of inspection. The inspectors will then descend to make significant and complex judgements about the school during a visit lasting less than two days.

They will convert the limited amount of evidence they've gathered into one of four blunt grades, two of which, 'inadequate' and 'requires improvement', can finish a head's career, damage the financial sustainability of the school, and make it difficult to recruit staff. But it's worse than that because being permanently 'Ofsted ready' is insidious. It results in school conversations that are dominated by the need to satisfy the Ofsted framework, rather than the need to improve the education of students. All this comes at a cost, and tragically, it is a very human one. The stress caused by the pressure of an impending inspection or downgrade has even, sadly, been linked to a number of teacher suicides.

There is a serious and urgent need to explore alternative methods of accountability, and I say, 'Let us look no further than Finland', which is not something I find myself saying every day. Finnish schools have a low accountability model. School inspections were abolished in the early 1990s, there are no national tests for pupils and school exam results are not published. You may well be thinking, what sort of *laissez-faire* madness is that? Surely a lack of accountability will encourage indifferent teaching, a blasé attitude towards learning, and the result will be poor achievement?

Not so. Finland is consistently ranked near the very top of the international league tables, it has a very high student life-satisfaction score and there is little difference in the performance between schools across the country. As this represents the holy grail, the impossible dream and a crock of gold all rolled into one for our own Department of Education, I respectfully request that they get their arses in gear and go take a closer look at Finland, because it is support, not inspection, that nurtures great schools.

After many years under the Ofsted yoke, I am conditioned to feel hyper-accountable for all of my actions. After writing this, I was genuinely concerned that an Ofsted rapid response team might be winging its way down from central office with the singular task of downgrading us.

However, way back in 2002, what did we care? We were good with outstanding features, don't you know, and we put up a massive PVC banner to make sure that everyone else knew about it too, particularly the two neighbouring schools, which had been graded satisfactory.

APRIL 2002:
I AM VERY MUCH LOOKING FORWARD TO WORKING WITH YOU

As the country was gearing up to celebrate the Queen's Golden Jubilee, I took the next step on my blossoming march towards headship by applying for a Head of Sixth Form job back at Caroline's old school. I edged the interviews, ahead of a very popular and competent in-house Deputy Head of Sixth called Kate Monks, who had been widely regarded as a shoe-in. I only realized how problematic this was going to be when, immediately after I'd accepted the job, the Head insisted I give my vanquished rival and now new colleague a pep talk. I was reluctantly escorted to a darkened room and shoved through the door, where I found Kate surrounded by close colleagues who were unsuccessfully trying to console her. What the Head thought I could possibly say to raise her spirits in this moment of disappointment I could not imagine.

Feeling slightly bullish at having been thrust into this uncomfortable situation, I toyed with the idea of saying, 'In the end, it's all about the students, and they are the winners here today, Kate, because they have ended up not only with the best candidate, but the second best one as well.' Or even,

'Never mind, I've heard there's a Head of Sixth job coming up soon at a school down the road.'

But as neither of these were appropriate, in the end I rather lamely said, 'I know you must be extremely disappointed at the moment, but I'm very much looking forward to working with you.' I thought this showed both understanding and optimism but I could immediately tell that 'extremely disappointed' was a gross understatement, and I wasn't convinced Kate was looking forward to working with me at all. As I beat a hasty retreat, I had real misgivings about how well we were going to get along together. In the end it turned out not to be a problem at all as Kate was highly professional and extremely capable, and together we found a way to rub along effectively. However, it may have been my paranoia, but I got the strong feeling that it wasn't just Kate's disappointment I had to contend with, but a fair number of other staff who also felt the Head had made the wrong choice.

This real or imagined resentment towards my leadership was compounded by a number of other awkward complications. I had joined part way through the year, so they needed me to pick up the geography classes that the outgoing Head of Sixth had relinquished and I was therefore forced to teach a subject I knew nothing about. I really was a complete liability because as well as not having a clue about geography and being unable to answer the simplest of student questions, I had to lean heavily on the other geography staff for support and resources.

Just when I could have really done with some domestic stability to help ground me for the challenges of my new role, our home situation went pear-shaped. The builders adding an extension to our cottage encountered structural issues with the roof, and we had to move out immediately until they could be resolved. We hurriedly decamped into a rented property in a neighbouring village, but unfortunately this turned out to have infrastructure problems all of its own.

The house was the last in the village at the bottom of a hill and, two weeks into our rental, the sewage outlet for the village got blocked and waste began backing up the hill. I came home late one Friday evening feeling a little beleaguered and demoralized at school, only to find raw sewage oozing across the front path from a blown manhole cover. I soon found myself ankle deep in excrement, desperately trying to stem a faecal tide. As I unhappily gagged to myself, I couldn't help but reflect that this was the perfect metaphor for my career move. It was starting to have an adverse effect on me – I wasn't sleeping so well and felt anxious at the thought of going to work. Not for the first time, I questioned whether I had made a terrible career mistake and seriously considered ringing up my previous Head to ask for my old job back. Also not for the first time, Caroline steadied the ship by telling me to hold my nerve and weather the storm.

I talked the situation through with Paul Bourdeaux and he reminded me about the 'zone of control' concept that he had covered during my training course in Falmouth. He pointed out that I could not control any of the staff perceptions of me prior to starting, so I needed to focus on the things I could control going forward. I followed his advice by putting all my efforts into developing positive relations with as many staff as possible, supporters and detractors alike. In addition, I worked ridiculously hard, remained completely professional and volunteered to help others out at every opportunity. Although this was exhausting, bit by bit, as the term progressed, I managed to start bringing staff over to my corner. By the end of term things began to feel considerably more positive for both myself and Kate, who had deservedly secured the Head of Sixth job that came up down the road. I appointed a bright, bubbly young psychology teacher called Michelle Nineham as her replacement. What she lacked in experience she made up for with an infectious enthusiasm and it wasn't long before the initial teething problems I had experienced seemed like a bad memory. I had learnt the important lesson that sometimes you just have to put your head down and ride these things out. To round things off, in September I finally got to ditch the geography lessons and resume science teaching, and in an ironic twist of fate, I discovered that as Mr Hodin was a sixth form tutor, I was now in charge of him. It took a will of iron not to tell him to sharpen up a bit.

SEPTEMBER 2002:

BEHAVE YOURSELVES

The question of whether children's behaviour has got worse over the years is a perennial debate. However, children nowadays are self-indulgent; they gobble up sweets and prefer gossip to exercise. They have terrible manners, they argue with their parents, they are contemptuous of authority and have little respect for their teachers. No, not my words, but those of the Greek philosopher Socrates from two and a half thousand years ago, indicating that, even then, the youth of the day had attitude.

We found a group of our Year Nine students to be particularly challenging. They really struggled to access our standard curriculum and we really struggled to control their behaviour. They proved to be such a handful that Mr Hodin decided we would team-teach them and allotted two teachers to teach ten of the most problematic students in a small group. One of those teachers was a battle-hardened, no-nonsense chemistry teacher called Val. The other was me. Officially the group was named XY3, but unofficially we called them all sorts of colourful names.

Luckily, because I was the Head of Sixth Form and a member of the Senior Leadership Team, these students knew they would need to moderate their behaviour in my presence. This delusion was rudely shattered on my arrival to my very first lesson, when a scrap of a girl called Chantelle

Roberts looked me up and down before turning to Val and shouting, 'Hey Miss, who the f*** is this dipstick?'

We found it very difficult to keep them all in the room at the same time. During one of our lessons, a boy called Darren Denton arrived late and proceeded to stare at us through the glass panel in the door. When one of us went over to tell him to come in, he would run off. A few minutes later he would come back, and we would repeat the sequence. After this had happened half a dozen times, I decided I would chase after him. I opened the door, burst out, and he ran off with me in hot pursuit. Round and round the school we went and, throughout the chase, for some inexplicable reason, he made the noise of a fire engine. As well as disturbing the whole school, we passed a group of parents of prospective students. I heard it later, on good authority, that Darren had helped them make up their minds about the suitability of our school for their offspring. I finally managed to corner him in the boys' toilet, but he refused to come out of the cubicle and instead set light to a toilet roll. This sort of incident was par for the course with XY3.

It would take absolutely nothing to set them off: loud noises, a flickering light, a visitor or, most notably, the weather. There is a perennial theory in schools that the wind makes children more excitable, even wild. I recently read about a study that tested this theory. It concluded that there was indeed a discernible change in behaviour with weather; however, it wasn't just the wind that caused this but any changes in the prevailing weather conditions. This was clearly manifest with XY3: the slightest bit of wind, rain, hail, thunder, lightning or snow would turn them into berserkers. There was only one more potent trigger for wild behaviour with XY3, and that was the appearance of Mrs Tibbles, a local cat.

Most of the time Mrs Tibbles enjoyed the love and attention she received from the students. Cooing, strokes, cuddles and treats were all on tap, but this had to be weighed up against the risk of being caught by XY3. If they got their hands on her they would squabble and fight over who got to hold her, and this would result in extreme handling – anything from a yanked tail or pulled legs to being dropped or becoming involved in a tug of war.

If, during a lesson, Mrs Tibbles was spotted ambling past the window, the class would erupt and, before we could secure the door, half of the group would have escaped to chase her down. Initially, I used to worry about how our lack of control would be seen by other teachers, but I needn't have worried as, one day, during my free lesson, the Head came running down the corridor towards me. 'Have you seen XY3?' he panted. 'They've run off out of my lesson. They said something about having to see a Mrs Tibbles. I think she must be the new supply teacher.'

Keeping them in the room was only half the problem. Once in, they were dangerous. They would dare each other to drink acid, whack each other with tripods and Darren would light the gas taps so that jets of flame would shoot out across the desk. Even the safety equipment was misused, as they loved to ping the elastic string of the safety googles so that it painfully twanged the neck of a classmate.

The strange thing about XY3, however, was that for all the chaos, they brought out the best in Val and me. They say that necessity is the mother of invention – well, XY3 was the mother of all necessities. If we didn't plan meticulously, differentiate for all ten of them or a have plan B, C, D and E, then all hell would break loose. This element of risk meant that we produced the most detailed, interesting and creative lessons. Not only that, but we got a lot more satisfaction from a good lesson with XY3 than we did with our other classes.

They differed significantly from other students in that they didn't take the conflict personally; they saw it as routine, part and parcel of school, and they held no grudges. If they saw me out of school, they seemed genuinely pleased to see me. They would wave, come over to say hello, and even introduce me to their families. Chantelle Roberts once served my family in a little tearoom she worked at. I was apprehensive about how it would pan out, but she went out of her way to look after us and did so with charm and the complete absence of expletives. I'm not sure whether it was a case of rose-tinted glasses, but when they moved on into Year Ten, Val and I experienced a hint of loss. It didn't last for long, though; we were soon distracted by the new XY3.

Several years later, I lit a bonfire at the end of my garden to burn off some garden waste. Now, I will admit it was slightly smokier than desired, but for one of my neighbours to ring the fire brigade was completely alarmist. When the fire engine arrived, there was a knock at the door, and when I opened it the fireman standing in front of me was none other than Darren Denton.

He very politely pointed out that the smoke from my fire was billowing out across the road and causing a traffic hazard. After helping me to extinguish the blaze, he gave me several useful tips on how not to cause a nuisance fire (oh, the irony!) before he shook my hand, thanked me for teaching him science all those years ago, and nonchalantly drove off.

I have since met several other students from XY3 in a variety of roles, and they were similarly professional and polite. The only conclusion I can draw from this is that bad behaviour in adolescence is not necessarily a true indicator of future character. I sort of knew this all along, really; after all, I was excluded three times myself.

Running a sixth form is really like being in charge of a school within a school, so I gained some very valuable leadership experience in the post. After two years I took the next obvious step on my mission to become a head by applying to be a deputy head at a city secondary school.

SEPTEMBER 2004:
STAPLES OR DRAWING PINS

On the morning of the interview, I joined four other interviewees making small talk around a tea urn. We were patiently waiting for the final candidate to arrive when, suddenly, the door burst open and the overdue person stumbled noisily into the room. Glasses askew, this dishevelled, well-spoken man apologized profusely to everyone for his tardiness before vigorously shaking the hands of each of us in turn. During the process, he managed to knock over a cup of coffee and step on my foot.

I wondered who on earth this eccentric whirlwind of a man was. Little did I know that he was destined to play a significant role in my future career. He introduced himself as Mr James Gregory, the current Head of English at the school. Given he was the only internal candidate, I was intrigued to find out how he had managed to arrive so late to the interview.

'I mean, it wasn't like you could pretend you got lost on the way in,' I teased. When he admitted that it was partly because he'd not read the schedule properly, and partly because he'd rushed back home because he'd forgotten his tie, I assessed his level of threat as a competitor to be medium to low. However, when I got chatting with him between tasks, I found myself increasingly invigorated by his boundless optimism and beguiling humour. When our brief discussions also revealed a razor-sharp mind, I raised his threat level to high. He openly shared his insights into the school with all of us, and this refreshing honesty was probably his undoing, as it took away his insider advantage. When I finally triumphed, he was the first to congratulate me, and he did so with genuine warmth and enthusiasm. It was a generosity of spirit that I would get to witness many times in the future.

We were not natural bedfellows; he was a public school, wine-loving chap who mainly enjoyed dinner parties and comfortable chairs. I was more of your state school, beans-on-toast kind of guy who mainly enjoyed outdoor mud-based activities.

However, when it came to talk about education, just like dolphins, we clicked. Once I took up the post, what started as a few casual end-of-the-day conversations about school, rapidly developed into regular, passionate and extended educational debates.

We discussed and questioned all manner of policy and practice: what was wrong with what we were doing; what we would change; what we would do if we were the Head. We acted as both sparring partner and sounding board for each other, and out of this hothouse of debate, the foundations of our future educational philosophy were laid. I realized much later that it was the many hours we had spent thrashing out our ideas in the trenches that helped prepare us for the challenges ahead.

I thought that being Head of Sixth Form had been a busy job, but that was because I had never been a deputy head before. During my first few weeks I was swamped by a stream of staff coming to see me. Some had legitimate problems that required my superior intellect, but many had questions I deemed 'urgent but not important'. They were urgent because the questioner was standing in my office expecting an answer; they were not important because I felt they were not at the strategic level my elevated status warranted. Here are some of the questions I was asked during that period:

* Should I use staples or drawing pins on the corridor noticeboards?
* Do the clocks go back or forwards in the spring?
* What was the original colour of this building?
* Can you recommend a chiropodist?
* What time is high tide?
* What do you think this rash is?

Why were they bothering me with this trivia? Did they not understand how important and busy I was? With time I came to realize that they were not really interested in the answers to these questions, which is lucky because I didn't know any of them other than that I think the rash was scabies. No, the questions were a front for secondary, much more important ones. They wanted advice on things like staffing issues, their domestic situation, future job opportunities, or they just wanted an excuse to size up the new deputy. Oblivious to this subtlety, I was concerned that all these interruptions were stopping me from getting anything useful done, and my solution was to put an opaque strip on my door window, so people were unable to see if I was free. This rather efficiently reduced the number of trivial questions I received, but at the same time prevented me from hearing those more important secondary ones as well. It was only later, when the truth dawned on me, that I removed my shield and became a little more useful to staff.

There was, however, one rather persistent staff visitor who only ever asked inconsequential questions. She totally ignored my opaque barrier and would burst into my office without knocking. Once, she did this while I was grabbing a late lunch. My food-laden fork was in the midway position between the plate and my mouth when she launched into an obscure query about staff parking. I deliberately held my fork in this position for the whole of the conversation, hoping to shame her into letting me eat my lunch, or, at the very least, finish that mouthful. Sadly, she continued regardless for about ten minutes, and I only got to take that cold, coveted mouthful after I had clarified the rationale behind our parking bays. I subsequently realized that I could gain a few seconds warning of her imminent arrival because I could see her hair approaching above my opaque shield. If I was quick, I could grab the phone and, when she entered, mouth something like 'Chair of Governors', before apologetically waving her on her merry way. Well, I was now a very important and busy person.

Deputy headship is a substantial role, and not only did everyone want a piece of me, but I was also in charge when the Head was out of school. I'm not sure how I skipped over this aspect of the job when I applied – after all, there's a big clue in the job title – but being solely in charge, even for short bursts, came as a bit of a shock. I quickly discovered I knew very little about a whole range of major issues such as finance, law, admissions, local politics, governance, health and safety, etc.

As a consequence, I once again found myself questioning whether I had bitten off more than I could chew. I wondered whether this was the 'Peter Principle' I had read about in one of my management books. This principle observes that people in a hierarchy tend to rise to their 'level of incompetence'. In other words, an employee is promoted based on their success in previous jobs until they reach a level (plateau) at which they are no longer competent. They then fester incompetently at that level as they are not good enough to move up any further. Perhaps I had arrived at my own 'Peter's Plateau'. All the deputy heads I had met previously were mature, considered and responsible. They were individuals of real substance; the sort of people you could rely on in an emergency. I really didn't feel like one of them at all; my brain seemed to be the same immature one I'd had at university. My body had aged but my brain seemed to have experienced a form of arrested development.

However, despite my private worries, the staff and students appeared to be taking me seriously and, as I had made it to half-term without being rumbled, I decided the best course of action was to continue to pretend I knew what I was doing. I went for the classic swan approach – in public I was outwardly calm and in control; behind the scenes, just like a swan's feet going nineteen to the dozen, I worked like mad to learn my trade. With every challenge I met, every issue I resolved and every school event that went smoothly, my confidence slowly grew. My mindset started to shift, so that not only did I believe I could cope with this job, but I began to believe that perhaps I could even cope with the big one as well. After receiving a fulsome round of applause from parents after an open-evening speech, where I was standing in for the Head, I was on a high.

FEBRUARY 2006:
BREATHING TOO LOUDLY

Being a teacher frequently requires you to maintain a straight face and toe the party line even though your natural response might be one of amusement. An example of this was when, shortly into the spring term, I found a new Year

Seven child sobbing in the corridor outside my office. Once I had managed to stem the flow of tears, I was able to identify the cause of the upset. The girl was really worried because she had been given a yellow behaviour slip, a low-level sanction in our behaviour management system. On closer examination there were two obvious issues. The crime she had committed was listed as 'breathing too loudly in the corridor' and it had been signed by a 'Miss Demeanour'.

On further investigation I identified the culprit, a spirited Year Nine student called Georgie Hendy. It turned out that she had managed to get her hands on a pad of these slips and had been dishing them out to the Year Sevens for a range of ridiculous offences: wearing sensible shoes; arriving early to lessons; having a Pokémon backpack; reading in the library at lunchtime. Most Year Sevens had ignored the slips, but the girl in my office had taken it to heart. I called Georgie into my office and hauled her over the coals for about five minutes, after which she said, 'Fair enough, Sir, but I didn't think any of them would take it seriously, and you've got to admit, it was a little bit funny, wasn't it?'

Outwardly I assumed an expression of outrage; inwardly I admitted it was a little bit funny. My sanction for Georgie was to mentor the little Year Seven she had upset, an arrangement that turned out to do both of them the world of good. Having to be responsible for a Year Seven, especially a delicate one, seemed to have a stabilizing effect on Georgie, at least for a short while.

The next time the Year Seven girl came to my attention was later that year when she took part in the school production of *Oliver*. She looked happy and confident and bore no resemblance to the timid mouse I had met previously, so it looked like Georgie's mentoring might have made a difference. Peer-to-peer mentoring is not always successful, as it is dependent on the mentee having a degree of respect for their mentor. The mentor may be given this respect because they are successful at school themselves: for example, because they are academically able, are the captain of a sports team, have a lead role in a play, or, as in the case of Georgie, they are the leader of a social circle.

The more similar the mentor is to their mentee the better, because they have much more credibility if they have had the same experiences and can speak the same language. I found this was also true of our guest speakers. We had regularly brought in successful individuals to inspire our students: Olympians, surgeons, politicians, writers, etc., but counter-intuitively, the more successful they were, the fewer students they inspired. Most students would appreciate the success of these high achievers, but also failed to be personally inspired because they simply concluded these people were a different breed to them. They could not visualize doing something similar because this stretched the elastic band of aspiration too far, and it snapped.

After one immensely stimulating talk from a top female judge, I enthusiastically asked some girls whether they felt inspired, and was taken aback when one simply said, 'Yeah, she was great, Sir, but people like us don't become people like that.' In light of this response, I changed tack and started to bring in many more ex-students as speakers. These seemed to have a far greater influence on our students because when they saw someone from their own school being successful, someone like them, they believed it was possible to do the same. These ex-students were much more popular and were always inundated with questions and swamped by students wanting to talk to them afterwards.

The dynamics of mentoring had played out similarly in my own career. I had had enormous respect for mentors like Miss Hussain and Paul Bourdeaux, who were not only successful at what they did, but were also like me. Consequently, I listened very carefully to their advice and acted upon it. I paid considerably less attention to some of the School Improvement Partners (SIPs) foisted upon me by the local authority once I became a head. Their role was to support, challenge and mentor headteachers, but not only had some of these mentors never run a successful school themselves, they were not like me at all. They were immensely interested in the parts of the job I liked the least: finance, health and safety, and policies. My strategy was always to make them welcome, to be very polite and agree with everything they suggested, but, when they had gone, I would file their action plans in the bottom drawer of my filing cabinet. As these advisors were replaced at such an alarming rate, this approach worked well because it meant that nobody really knew what I was doing, and this gave me the freedom to do my own thing without causing too much upset.

Later in my career I discovered that mentoring your own staff is one of the most rewarding roles you can play as a headteacher. Guiding people, helping them grow and encouraging their development is an incredibly generative experience. Not only do you get to share in their successes, but it costs nothing more than a little bit of your time.

MAY 2006:
FORTY WINKS

I was lucky enough to be given the chance to visit China in the summer term as part of a local authority cultural and educational exchange. Ten of us, a mix of local officials, advisors and teachers, flew to Shanghai to examine the Chinese education system. The trip was a real eye-opener, as China's economy was beginning to boom and their investment in education was phenomenal. We visited a string of newly built schools, all of which dwarfed anything we had back in the UK. The first primary school we visited had three thousand students on roll and a building that would have put the headquarters of most medium-sized European companies to shame. Some information must have got lost in translation because, for unknown reasons, our hosts believed us to be top Western educational experts. We were given the red-carpet treatment everywhere we went, and film crews and photographers followed us as we shook hands and drank tea with local dignitaries. We were truly not worthy of such honour, but because we were enjoying it so much, we all agreed it would be rude to challenge this misconception at such a late stage.

Looking abroad for educational inspiration is a path well worn by governments seeking to rise up the international league tables. Countries that perform well in the OECD-PISA tests (Program for International Student Assessment) receive a swarm of visitors from other nations looking for the magic ingredient to take back home. In recent years, the education systems of Finland and East Asia have been among those most visited, and this was partly the reason why we were in China. The problem with this type of smash and grab approach is that the success of an education system cannot be distilled down to a particular way of teaching or the range of subjects in its curriculum, and we immediately noticed two significant differences between the experience of Chinese and UK teachers.

Firstly, the contact time the Chinese teachers had with their students was sometimes as low as 40 per cent – just two lessons in front of the students per day compared with the four-to-five-lesson slog common in the UK. We were completely envious of this, as it meant their teachers had built-in time for preparing lessons, department planning, lesson observation and all the things UK teachers must squeeze in over and above a busy day's teaching. This low contact time also allowed for a much faster turnaround on marking and assessment, which enabled them to deliver more responsive teaching and personalized feedback. We often saw small groups of students meeting their teachers out of formal lesson time, in breakout groups or individually, to review material and ensure their mastery of the subject.

Secondly, and even more significant than this extra preparation time, were the high expectations of children expressed by the government, their teachers, parents and communities. On our visit we observed a very positive attitude to school; teachers were held in high esteem and education was seen as precious and valuable by the children and their parents. As a result, we saw things that we were unlikely to see in the UK. For example, I witnessed one teacher effectively teach a class of over ninety students because they were impeccably behaved and on task throughout. I talked to one head who was on an evening visit to the home of a child who was misbehaving. He told me that he had invited all the relatives to the meeting, which would be regarded as a shameful event by the whole family. In the canteen I saw tutors making formal notes on what and how much their students ate for lunch, so they could report this back to parents.

Now, it's not that I wanted to return home and watch my students chomp down their turkey twizzlers or, even less palatable, pop in for an evening meal with their families, but it was the fact they could do these things that emphasized real differences in culture. These differences mean that simply copying a teaching method from another country will not necessarily lead to the UK rocketing up the league tables.

When the 2012 PISA tables for maths were published, the DfE were understandably aghast to see the UK languishing in 26th position. We were way behind Shanghai, whose lead was so clear that the OECD estimated their results were the equivalent of its students having had three additional years of schooling. The DfE suddenly became very interested in the method of maths teaching in Shanghai, where their whole-class teaching approach, known as 'maths mastery', was very different to the UK's more child-centred model. With good intentions, they invested £74 million in order to import this Shanghai-style maths mastery teaching to UK primary schools. However, our cultural and social context is so very different from what we witnessed in Shanghai that, without addressing some of the background issues, like behaviour, lack of parental support and teacher contact time etc., this type of copycat initiative is unlikely to deliver the magic bullet the government is looking for. As yet, the introduction of maths mastery has yet to deliver its hoped-for gains.

The only innovation I did try to bring back to my school was an afternoon nap for teachers. In one school we visited, I was shown a room adjacent to the staffroom full of mini beds where staff could grab a quick forty winks after lunch. I pleaded with my Head for our own set of mini beds, trying to sell it as a mass version of the Maggie Thatcher power-nap, but she didn't buy it. Nowadays, however, if I'm caught snoozing in the afternoon, I explain that the practice is based on one of the most successful education systems in the world.

On our last day the students put on a cultural evening for us. It was most enjoyable; the performances were of the highest quality with singing and dancing accompanied by traditional Chinese instruments. At the end of the evening, we were called up onto the stage for what we assumed was a final presentation. We were confused when there was no presentation forthcoming, but rather the audience was staring at us in eager anticipation. To our horror, our host explained that they were expecting us to respond with a short performance of our own. Had we not read his email? It seems that in an ironic twist of fate this message had got lost in translation. Under intense scrutiny, and with no real time for a considered discussion, we ended up subjecting them to an excruciating version of 'Swing Low Sweet Chariot', most of which we hummed because we only knew the words to the chorus. When we had finished, there was a good twenty seconds of stunned silence before a ripple of polite applause broke out, after which we bolted for the airport.

JULY 2006:
THE ART OF DELEGATION

As Deputy Head, I was slowly learning how to delegate effectively, but it was a work in progress. I found that I was still a little too enamoured by my way of doing things and worried that if I passed the ball to someone else, they might run off in the wrong direction or drop it. President Eisenhower once said, 'Leadership is the art of getting someone else to do something you want done, because they want to do it.' Wise words, but this requires careful thought, planning and finesse, none of which were in evidence during a situation that arose on the afternoon of our summer fair.

This event took place on the front field, with stalls run by the students, staff and the parent–teacher association. There were stalls selling pick and mix, cookies and candyfloss, all guaranteed to deliver the desired glucose rush, alongside a smattering of old favourites such as tombola, splat the rat, hoopla, etc. By mid-afternoon, things appeared to be running smoothly, so I retired to my office for a brief rest. It was during this break that a lapse in supervision at the front gate enabled a small group of undesirables to sneak onto the site.

Suddenly, Mr Dunk, the Assistant Head, appeared panting at my door telling me to come quickly, as a group of boys from a neighbouring school were wandering around the building. I carefully considered this information before deciding that now might be a good time to delegate, but I realized this wasn't going to be easy because Mr Dunk was a 'Slopey Shoulders' – the third of my big five teaching beasts.

These slick charmers are members of the Senior Leadership Team who love the power their position affords them but employ a hands-off approach to management. They are on the Senior Leadership Team in name only, as they do not lead, and they certainly do not engage in teamwork. They will often go 'missing in action' by fading into the background at the first sign of a difficult parent or staffing conflict. They sneak off early from evening events and are very difficult to locate during an emergency. If challenged on their lack of engagement, their default response is to say, 'I'm sorry, but that is way beyond my pay grade.'

Conversely, they are also keen to falsely promote an image that they are working very hard by saying things like, 'I brought in an apple three days ago, but I've been so busy that I just haven't had time to eat it yet.'

They tend to spend most of their time in their offices, preferring to ping out hundreds of highlighted memos rather than talk to members of staff face to face. In essence, they have completely forgotten that there is a good reason why they get paid more, teach less, and have an office and a title.

Unless you work closely with these individuals you wouldn't know just how flaky they are because they are masters of schmooze. Using a potent combination of insincere compliments and phrases they've learnt from their latest management course, they dupe people into doing their work for them. They say things like:

'You know, I have always had the greatest respect for your work as a head of department. I think some of what you do is of national importance, and it's absolutely criminal that it's not shared more widely. I'm sorry you don't currently agree with what I'm saying, but I really hope that just for now, after recontextualizing, you will deploy these mission-critical process-centric methodologies for me.'

Not only are they masters of this type of downward delegation, but they are also skilled in the art of the upward offload, which was exactly what Mr Dunk was doing when he came into my office and threw me this hospital pass.

'Well, Mr Dunk,' I replied, 'why don't you go back and tell them in no uncertain terms that they need to leave? I'm sure they will. Just be firm, you know, show them who's boss.'

'They definitely won't. They're not scared of me at all. When I spoke to them, they told me to f-off. That's why I'm here,' he replied.

'Mmm, I really need you to deal with this. You've caught me right in the middle of something quite important,' I replied.

'Well, I don't think this sort of thing is covered in my job description,' he said defensively.

'I think you'll find it's under the section that says, "and any other reasonable task requested by the Headteacher",' I fired back.

'Well, you're not the Headteacher are you, and this is way beyond my pay grade, so you really need to sort it out; otherwise I think someone is going to get hurt,' he insisted.

I contemplated offering to do his bus duty for the rest of the term if he made the problem go away, but I realized this would be pitiful, so I grabbed my jacket and apprehensively followed old Slopey Shoulders out of the door.

On the way to meet the trespassers, I thought to myself, why involve me? I was more brains than brawn and absolutely no use to anyone in a scrap. They were unlikely to be scared off by a short, bespectacled man with a squeaky voice. Sure enough, they weren't. They refused to leave and, when I insisted they did, things turned nasty. A physical altercation was only avoided when, in the nick of time, several other teachers arrived along with Mr Gregory, who loudly informed me that the police were on their way. We escorted the group of youths off the premises, and this would have been a job well done had not the ringleader, as a parting shot, calmly whispered in my ear that he would be waiting for me after school to give me a good stabbing.

This was not the type of community interaction I had been hoping to foster, so I was very grateful that the police, who attended the incident, hung around long enough to see me safely off-site later that afternoon. When I returned to school the next morning, it was to Armageddon. The front entrance was blocked by the burnt-out remains of a stolen car that had been deliberately driven into our front gates and set on fire. School windows were smashed and the slates from a whole section of our roof had been thrown onto the field. The CCTV footage clearly showed it was our visitor and his friends from earlier, so I was mightily relieved to be told later that day that he had been arrested.

It had been only a decade earlier that Philip Lawrence, a secondary headteacher and father of four, died after being stabbed outside his west London school while protecting a pupil who was being assaulted. His death had left an indelible mark on the consciousness of teachers across the country, and although no one had come to any harm in our own episode, it was an unwelcome and unsettling reminder that the complex problem of serious youth violence continued to lurk just beyond the school gates.

SEPTEMBER 2006:
EMOTIONAL RIPPLES

When I was at school a small, bearded teacher called Dr Smith taught us biology. He was the very worst type of teacher because of his unpredictability. In some lessons he was sweetness and light, whereas in others he would explode with unparalleled ferocity. We could never relax because even if the lesson seemed to be going well, we never knew when he might turn. The smallest things could trigger his fury: a lid not replaced on a marker pen, a wasted sheet of A3 or a student arriving late. He was actually a very good teacher, but when he blew, he blew big and it really was a hideous experience for his victim, albeit compulsive viewing for everyone else.

I was also called Dr Smith, I also taught biology and I had also moved to Cornwall for a new job. I was very keen for the resemblance to end right there, and unsurprisingly, so was Caroline. Consequently, I have always tried my hardest to keep my emotions at work on an even keel. Over the years I have endeavoured to remain upbeat even in emotionally charged situations, of which there were plenty during this autumn term – I was shouted at by angry parents, we struggled to balance the budget and I found out that a cherished member of staff was seriously ill.

I had already developed a few strategies to help maintain my mental health generally, and these were helpful when faced with such a succession of difficult challenges. As it has been well documented that the physical markers of stress, like heart rate and blood pressure, tend to go down in rural environments, I went walking in the country or by the coast as often as I could. This had the additional benefit of me often not being able to get a signal, and thus ensured I was properly disconnected. To help me deal with an array of different issues, I had also developed a technique of visually minimizing them, as you would a page on a computer screen. The issues would sit as harmless minimized icons in my mind's eye until I needed to maximize them again. I found this helped prevent me from becoming overwhelmed.

During these emotionally challenging situations I tried really hard to ensure that my voice and demeanour were not an accurate reflection of the emotional conflict going on inside my head. The worst leaders I have worked under have been unable to master this, and so their prevailing mood constantly affects the atmosphere of the school. They transfer their mood to others and create emotional waves that ripple out through the whole organisation. The tell-tale sign you have this sort of leader is if the first question everyone asks when they arrive in the morning is, 'What sort of mood are they in today?'

While some leaders surround you with a shield of calm competence, this type of leader will take you on an emotional roller-coaster. Their temperamental lability generates an atmosphere of fear among the staff, who soon realize that at the drop of a hat, they could find themselves at the end of a hot-blooded tongue-lashing. Consequently, they will do their best to avoid these leaders if they can. One such leader I knew inadvertently advertised their prevailing mood by the speed at which they walked. The more irate they were, the faster they walked; and the faster they walked, the faster their shoes clacked on the hard wooden corridors, giving staff an early warning of both their approach and their frame of mind.

Clack . . . clack . . . clack . . . clack . . . clack (they were in a good mood).

Clack, clack, clack, clack, clack (not so good; best follow the lockdown procedure of run, hide, tell).

The victims of such emotional outbursts may themselves unconsciously react by snapping at other members of staff or by being sharp with the students in their next lesson, therefore unintentionally becoming the conduit by which this negative emotion ripples out through the school community.

Having observed the damaging effect of this leadership style, I vowed that if I ever became a head, I would do my utmost to remain calm and upbeat irrespective of what was going on behind the scenes. Staff need and deserve a degree of emotional stability and decorum from their leaders.

I later discovered that this is very much easier said than done.

JANUARY 2007:
TELEOLOGICAL

Two years after becoming a deputy head I attempted to fulfil my quest by going for the big one. An opportunity had arisen to become the Head of Torquay Girls'

Grammar School, and as I wasn't willing to let Peter and his Principle hold me back, I decided to give it a go.

The selection procedure took place over two gruelling days in January, and a particular highlight was the governors' buffet. On the first day I had capably risen to the challenge of working the coffee urn while under considerable pressure from a waiting queue. Those beverage urns can be devilishly difficult to operate; it's hard to know whether they're not pouring because they're empty or because you don't have the knack. I was hoping that my confident push on the top plunger had been noted by all. The buffet was a higher level of challenge still. I'm sure the event was designed as an innocent mingle, but for the interviewees it was a sort of frenetic gastronomic speed date.

Believing (correctly) that every move I made was being judged, even selecting a plate of buffet food felt like a test. I needed to choose enough to look hearty but not so much that I looked greedy. Anything that was difficult to eat, like chicken wings or a cream slice, was a no-no. This imagined scrutiny affected my decision-making, and I ended up with two mini pork pies, a mini baguette without any butter, a beetroot salad and a slice of cherry pie all on the same plate.

The format was for the candidates to sit down with a governor, talk for about five minutes and then rotate around the table to another governor. It is not humanly possible to eat and sell yourself in such a short time span, so I found myself talking continuously for the five minutes with each governor before vigorously stuffing my mouth full of food and chewing really quickly during the transitions. While I was charming everyone with this approach, my tie happily flapped between my beetroot salad and cherry pie as a prelude to smearing a bright red montage onto my white shirt. I only noticed this shirt carnage minutes before I was about to give my big pitch to a hall full of staff and governors. However, despite looking like I had been involved in a violent altercation, or maybe even because of it, to my surprise I was offered the job. It is entirely possible this was because some of the more astute governors had been unable to attend the interviews and/or the panel were blown away by my offer to get involved with the Duke of Edinburgh Award scheme – either way they chose me.

Bingo, hurrah, hallelujah or, as that madcap Scottish comedy duo the Krankies would say, fan-dabby-dozy. Or not, as the case may be. Rather disappointingly, my euphoria at realizing a goal fifteen years in the making was short-lived. It lasted as long as it took to tell all my family and friends that I had got the job, after which I felt a little bit empty. Luckily, we had covered this 'post-goal achievement' scenario on the self-esteem course. The theory is that humans are teleological, goal orientated – happy when they have a goal or target to achieve. I had enjoyed the sense of direction and purpose of the journey, especially when my brain gave me a lovely dopamine hit every time I reached a milestone. Now I had reached the target, the sense of purpose had gone, and the dopamine flow had dried up. I remember hearing Alex Ferguson, the famous football manager, describing how the joy of winning the Champions League only lasted a short while before he began to think about the next campaign. I was just like Alex Ferguson then, except of course that he was one of the greatest football managers of all time, and I wasn't.

After a short period of reflection, I worked on adjusting my mindset and resetting my goals. I began to think about just how I would steer my newly acquired ship in the right direction, to motivate its crew and to prepare for the storms ahead. In the process of doing this, I found myself becoming increasingly anxious. Had I really thought this through, or had I been over-enamoured with the idea of becoming a head rather than actually being one? Had my desire to make recompense for giving up medicine led me to be a touch hasty?

I began to worry about my readiness in purely practical terms. Among other things, I was unsure how to create a school development plan, I still had no real idea how to manage a school budget and was yet to get to grips with how the timetable worked. I was also unclear on the sort of image I wanted to project. Should I be upgrading my mobile to this new Apple iPhone everyone was talking about or part-exchange my tired old Peugeot for a BMW 3-Series? There were other issues too. On the domestic front, the school was over fifty miles from where we lived, and as this was not a good time for a family move, I had to rent a very sad and soulless modern flat in Torquay to stay in during the week.

Along with these practical problems, I also developed a creeping case of imposter syndrome as I began to question whether I was worthy. Did I really know what I was doing? Did I really understand the issues? Was I mature enough to make sensible decisions? Could I convince the staff and students to follow me? For the first time in my career there would be no one else to ask – the buck stopped with me. The stakes were high; education is precious, and I knew that if I messed up it could have detrimental effects on my students for the rest of their lives. Fortunately, this growing sense of trepidation was countered by feelings of excitement about finally being in charge. This was my big chance to do things my way, the chance to really make a difference, and perhaps even the chance to create something special. I was absolutely determined to give it my very best shot, so I spent the next few months furiously researching, planning and plotting the course ahead. In the end, none of this fully prepared me for what was to come. On 1 September 2007, the starting gun was fired, and I was instantly engulfed in the trials and tribulations of leading a school – a daily diet of blood and guts that I affectionately refer to as 'Head Trauma'.

Part Four: Headship I: The Compliant Years

SEPTEMBER 2007:
BLURRED VISION

In order to steer the ship, I needed to know where we were heading, but I was still a bit hazy on this. During the interview process, people were constantly pressing me on my vision for the school. I had prepared a suitable answer, having researched the online mission statements of other schools. I had discovered, not unsurprisingly, that there isn't a school mission statement in the world that does not have worthy aims or desirable goals. Unfortunately, they all merge into one big dollop of aspirational mush. For example, here is a 'one size fits all' mission statement I synthesized from my research.

> We respect the precious, unique and individual
> needs of our children and seek to nurture
> a caring environment that emphasizes the

social, emotional, environmental, physical, psychological, practical, intellectual, creative, compassionate, moral and ethical development of each and every child, none of whom will ever be left behind.

We want our students to have deep understanding and compassion for all others with the courage to act on their beliefs as enlightened and spiritual beings connected with the world around them, but also in touch with their inner selves and confident in the possession of their innate talents.

They will act with thoughtfulness and humanity, utilizing a rich awareness of their heritage so they can lead and serve in every sphere of human activity, fulfilling their incredible potential while most importantly being the architects of lives that transcend the ordinary at the same time as keeping their bedrooms tidy.

The absurdity of a school vision statement only really hit me when, shortly after my appointment, I was outlining my vision to some parents. Most of them nodded in general agreement, satisfied that I had at least thought about it. However, for one rather intense parent, this was not enough; she wanted to know precisely *when* I would achieve these aims. Would it be while her child was still at the school?

This really threw me, because the truthful answer was: 'We will never achieve them. Our aims are noble but absurd; they are well intentioned but impossible to achieve. They are stellar aspirations that we will forever work towards but never actually reach, and despite our best intentions there will always be someone left behind, and there is a real danger that someone may be your daughter.'

Rather than tell her this inconvenient truth, I speculatively answered, 'Maybe by my third year?' This seemed to placate her because she said that as her daughter was only in Year Seven, at least her final three years would be in a school that delivered on its mission statement.

A school's mission statement provides only a vague indication of its preferred direction of travel. It is not really designed to be scrutinized on a practical level, not least because the majority of students, their parents and indeed staff are unable to remember its aims, let alone articulate what they mean. Schools often try to overcome this issue by encapsulating their aims in a catchy positive motto like:

* Learn to love to learn.
* Everyone successful, every day.
* Building a better world, one student at a time.

Many schools go for a Latin motto, which seems to fly in the face of all sensible communication. Why try to encapsulate your mission in a language that has not been spoken for over a thousand years? It immediately requires translation into English, and then, because these statements are usually a bit cryptic, further analysis is required.

For example, one of the schools I worked at had the motto, *Sine Labe Decus*, which roughly translated means 'Honour without Dishonour'. I like to think of myself as a learned fellow, but for the life of me I have been unable to work out what this means. Surely, as you cannot have honour *with* dishonour, the 'without dishonour' bit is redundant? No one at the school was ever able to give me a satisfactory explanation for the meaning of the motto, so I imagine it was a daily nightmare for the person in charge of marketing.

If the motto of a school is supposed to be a mirror of what actually goes on, then I can suggest some alternatives. They are slightly less optimistic, but far more grounded in school reality, and I have kept the Latin vibe going:

* *Numquam in loco tempore* – Never knowingly in the right place at the right time.
* *Canis cibum me Duis congue sem* – The dog ate my homework.
* *Non possum manum meam nec arari poterit claudere mitigatur tristitia erit super Domine*

foraminis – I cannot take my earring out
because the hole will close over, Sir.

I naively thought that improving a school would be easy, but the problem is, however clear your vision, it is very hard to make it a reality. Firstly, because the blood and guts of everyday school life gets in the way, and secondly, because government policy is built on shifting sands.

During my time as a head, I have served under seven different education secretaries, six of whom have not lasted two full years in post. This has not stopped each of them from trying to impose their vision of education upon schools. Such educational speed-dating is unmanageable, and I don't think it is arrogance to conclude that established headteachers might be better placed than these transients to know what is best for their students. What schools need are prolonged periods of stability instead of a never-ending ride on a policy-go-round. The control of education policy should be taken out of the hands of the government of the day and given to an independent body made up of employers, schools and colleges, universities, parents and teachers with a limited element of cross-party representation. This would help to end the continual political interference schools experience and would create a structure that could outlast any changes in government.

Any proposed changes in direction or operation should be consulted on, trialled and evaluated in good time.

Unfortunately, we have experienced the complete opposite from the DfE, whose Latin motto is *Mutatio est nostrum modo constant* – Change is our only constant.

OCTOBER 2007:
STAND UP STRAIGHT

The behaviour at the grammar school was not quite as I had imagined. It was not awful, but it wasn't how I wanted it to be. During my first assembly with Year Eleven, the students were unashamedly talking to each other while I was speaking, even though their Head of Year was hissing at them from the side of the hall to stop. I let it go for as long as I could, but it got to the point where, for the sake of my credibility, I had no option but to stop what I was saying and rebuke the whole year group.

This was a necessary but exceedingly awkward course of action, and far removed from the uplifting and positive message I had hoped to deliver. Later that same day, while popping into lessons to get a feel for the school, I had to take one of those Year Eleven students to task. I witnessed this student being rude to her physics teacher during an astronomy lesson when, as well as being generally disruptive, she shouted out the old classic, 'How big is Uranus, Miss?' I didn't feel I could let this go either, so I asked the student to step outside so that I could admonish her for her rudeness. In no particular order, I was expecting embarrassment, contrition and an apology to feature in her response. Instead, she just ranted at me.

'This is our school, not yours. You've only been here for five minutes; we've been here for five years. Things are fine as they are without you coming in and telling us off. Who do you think you are?'

'Well, I'm pretty sure I am the Headteacher, but I think you probably need to come down to my office, so I can clarify this for you,' was my snappy reply. I realized as she flounced off down the corridor in front of me that student behaviour was going to need some attention. Further investigation revealed that not only was the behaviour code vague, but it was inconsistently applied. In essence no one was clear what the rules were, and students received wildly differing sanctions from teachers for similar transgressions. This confusion caused a sense of injustice that often exacerbated the conflict.

There was a clear need for me to roll up my sleeves and get stuck into the not inconsiderable task of changing behaviour and expectations. Initially, after consultation with staff and students, this involved the creation of an agreed behaviour and uniform policy. Then staff training was needed to help embed the behaviours that facilitated learning and to establish what our boundaries were, along with clear accompanying sanctions and praise. This is all management speak for teaching students to be considerate of others, including teachers, so that we could all get on with learning.

Establishing a good level of behaviour in a school is a marathon rather than a sprint, and once achieved requires constant maintenance. It is only natural for hormonally fuelled teenagers to test out boundaries, so these need to be firmly and fairly reiterated on a regular basis. Later in the year, I concluded that we must have been making progress when, during an assembly, the Head of Year Eight spent a good ten minutes outlining the type of earrings compliant with our uniform code. She demonstrated that if you could get your little finger into a hooped earring while it was still on your ear, then it was too big. I reasoned that if she felt comfortable dedicating a whole assembly to this level of transgression, then most other things must be fine.

Expectations of behaviour have changed from the distant past. This was highlighted when a group of visiting old girls recounted some of the minor misdemeanours regarded as major crimes when they were at the school in the 1940s. If they were seen taking their beret off on the bus, buying an ice cream while still in uniform or walking on the wrong side of the corridor, they were clapped into detention. Talking during a lesson was such a heinous transgression that they were sent to stand in the entrance hall. Normally the entrance hall was strictly out of bounds to students, so standing there, alone and exposed, was torture. They would have to explain themselves to every passing member of staff, before inevitably it was the headmistress who passed by. Even now, decades later, returning old girls hover at the front door unsure if the 'no girls in the entrance hall' rule still applies. You can coax them across the threshold, but they remain jittery until they are escorted beyond its walls.

The old girls told me that in the past, great store was set on their deportment, the way they stood and walked. This seems an archaic expectation, but medical studies have shown that sitting and standing straight during adolescence can prevent all sorts of back issues later in life, so there was method in this ancient practice. Deportment involved more than just being able to sit and stand up straight; it was about moving around the school in a calm and considered manner, not running in the corridors or skidding around corners. Those students displaying outstanding achievement in this arena were awarded a deportment sash. By all accounts this was an extremely desirable item of attire, and the chosen few would sashay around the school to the envy of others. The old girls told me how they would practise walking upright by balancing piles of textbooks on their heads in an effort to gain a sash.

Once they had left, I decided to take a tour of the school to assess the current standards of deportment. I came across many students slouched in front of screens in a banana shape, with their spines slumped and backs unsupported. At lesson changeover students (and staff) barged noisily down corridors or shuffled along with heads down, backs bent, and, at one point, a student flew around a corner right into me. I came to the rapid conclusion that the reintroduction of the deportment sash was a non-starter.

JUNE 2008:
THE HEAD IS A LIGHTWEIGHT

During my first year, alongside improving behaviour, I felt the need to make some changes. I was keen to make my mark and be the breath of fresh air that moved the school swiftly onwards and upwards. So, I upgraded some of the school signage, organized a 'Curry and Quiz' night for parents and provided a tea lady in the staffroom, after staff persuaded me that this was guaranteed to pack it out – a service I subsequently withdrew due to lack of uptake. As I'm sure you will recognize, these were all 'non-urgent non-important' changes, and part of a suite of low-impact quick fixes. None of these actions produced any meaningful difference, and that is because all worthwhile change in schools takes considerably more time and effort than this – a conclusion supported by research published in the *Harvard Business Review* in 2017.

This research examined the effectiveness of different styles of leadership in UK academies. They identified five styles of leader, only one of which they felt was truly effective in the long term. The five leadership types were:

* The Philosophers – leaders who talk a good game, love to discuss teaching and learning, but have very little impact on the academic or financial performance of their school.

* The Surgeons – who make everything look great while they are in your employ. They clinically (some might say cynically) focus all the attention and resources on exam classes. After enhancing their own reputation with early gains, they usually leave before the school falls apart. Unsurprisingly, they are well thought of and highly paid.

* The Soldiers – leaders who like efficiency and order. They're tenacious, cost-cutting, task-focused leaders who trim everything back to the bone and make people work harder. They do improve the schools' long-term financial performance, but exam results stay the same.

* The Accountants – these try to grow their schools out of trouble. They systematically look for new revenue sources, such as acquiring a primary school. They can dramatically increase revenue, but examination results remain the same, as this is not their focus.

* The Architects – far rarer, more effective leaders, who quietly redesign their schools and transform the communities they serve.

> They take a holistic view of the school, its
> stakeholders and its role in society and believe
> schools only fail because they're poorly
> designed. They know it takes time to improve
> a school, so they take a long-term view of what
> they need to do. Unlike the Surgeons, theirs is
> the way of the tortoise, not the hare.

As I knew nothing of any of this at the time, I found myself looking around for a role model who would help me realize my dream of becoming a Heroic Head. The person who caught my eye was the much-lauded Sir Michael Wilshaw, Principal of the Mossbourne Academy in Hackney. After turning around a failing school in Newham and having great success with his new academy in one of London's most deprived boroughs, he had been described by the Shadow Education Secretary Michael Gove as a real hero. Having lived in Hackney myself, I knew it was a tough gig, so this guy must have something about him. I knew he was strong on discipline, liked a traditional curriculum and was very focused on raising achievement; not only that, but he had a quiet, understated manner that I identified with. He seemed to be a tailor-made role model. In retrospect, I should have delved a bit deeper and looked beyond the headlines because I would have discovered that I fundamentally disagreed with many of his views, including those insinuating that teachers are lazy, unprofessional and have no idea what stress is.

These controversial views became highly apparent when he subsequently went on to become the Head of Ofsted. However, as I was blissfully ignorant at the time, I aspired to be more like Sir Michael.

Unfortunately, an end-of-year parent survey confirmed there was still a lot of work to be done on my part in this respect, because after a series of questions about various aspects of the school, parents were asked if they had any other comments to make. One respondent simply wrote: 'Yes, the Head is a lightweight.' After less than one year in post, this seemed a bit harsh, so I redoubled my efforts to develop myself into more of a heavyweight.

OCTOBER 2008:
BUILDING FOR THE FUTURE

Our sixth form centre was located slightly off the main site and had originally been a modest manor house with stables. It might have been sturdy back in 1884, when it was built, but time had taken its toll and it was now in need of serious attention. It had a leaky roof, large patches of green mould climbing the inside walls and crumbling plasterwork. Despite this decay, the staff and students were very fond of it and had affectionately named it 'Mildew Manor'. Mrs Rumbold, who was the Head of Sixth Form, had her office there. She was a formidable lady who had taught at the school for over thirty years and was about to retire. She was an old-school, no-nonsense matriarch who taught classics, and she very nearly left us in spectacular fashion.

One afternoon, I received a phone message from the sixth form secretary saying there had been an incident and could I get down to the manor immediately. Slightly perturbed, I dashed down and entered the foyer, only to be met by a ghost. It was Mrs Rumbold and she had just had a near-death experience. She had been sitting at her desk drinking coffee when she had heard a crack above her head and, before she could react, the whole ceiling had collapsed on top of her. Miraculously she was unharmed. On hearing the commotion, the sixth form secretary had rushed over to help, only for a shaky Mrs Rumbold to emerge from her room covered in plaster dust and clutching a rubble-filled mug. Two passing sixth form girls asked her if she was okay.

'Yes, thank you, girls, I'm fine,' came Mrs Rumbold's curt reply before she added, 'Grace, that top you are wearing is not school uniform, please don't wear it again, and Julie, I am still expecting your essay on my desk by the end of the day.' Without breaking a sweat, she dusted herself down and strode across the foyer straight into her classics class to teach about the Roman invasion of Britain. I was impressed that despite the world literally collapsing around her, she was still focused on delivering the curriculum.

After a survey of the damage, the council declared that the manor needed significant structural repairs to keep it habitable. As it would be cheaper to build a brand-new sixth form building, that is exactly what we did, and the manor was put on notice. This was a shame because it had served our needs well over the years, but it had been built in a different era, for a different purpose, and was not really designed for the delivery of a twenty-first-century education.

This was also true of the school leadership arrangements I had inherited, and although, unlike the sixth form centre, I did not need to build a completely new structure, there was a definite need to blend the best elements of the old with my vision for the new. As I still carried the scars of my appointment to Head of Sixth Form, I was careful to instigate this transition sensitively and avoid alienating too many people. This involved an awful lot of groundwork. I needed to rearrange the roles and responsibilities of the senior team and persuade the key Heads of Department of the need for change. A head who wishes to introduce this sort of evolutionary change can be greatly assisted by having the chance to appoint his or her own people – people with a similar vision and drive, who are much more likely to buy into new plans as they will want to justify the faith placed in them. I was very lucky in this respect as I had already been able to appoint a very competent new deputy called Mr Charlwood in the summer before I joined the school. In addition, not only was I able to bring a dynamic biology teacher called Dr Halliday with me from my previous post, but when Mrs Rumbold retired, I got a major personal and professional boost when my former co-conspirator, James Gregory, also joined my team.

This combination of fortunes enabled me to start building a critical mass of like-minded people. I knew the tipping point had been reached when several of the more reticent non-believers started to show an interest in some of the changes we were making. I welcomed them on-board with open arms, as I had learnt over the years how important it is not to allow groups of staff to become marginalized. I therefore gradually began to surround myself with friendly faces.

NOVEMBER 2008:
HEALTH AND SAFETY

Mrs Rumbold's near-death experience highlighted to me just how dangerous the school environment can be. Even before we finally abandoned the Manor it managed to claim two more victims. A member of staff got electrocuted in its kitchen and one of our students fell down the main staircase; thankfully they both received minor injuries and recovered quickly.

Danger is inherent in the design and fabric of many of our old school buildings. However, by far the biggest danger posed to our students is the students themselves. There are a multitude of ways in which they will injure themselves.

They will slip on the slightest bit of ice, water or oil. They will trip over their bags, their laces, the carpet, and some will even trip over on thin air. They will accidently collide with friends, staff, visitors, open windows and goalposts. They bounce off trampolines at crazy angles, whack each other with their hockey sticks, scald themselves while cooking and super-glue their fingers together. They will routinely dislocate limbs, bruise soft tissues and swallow inanimate objects.

This accumulation of accidents can become overwhelming if not kept in check. Luckily, standing between our students and total carnage is the governors' health and safety committee. This erstwhile body has the remit to evaluate any hazards and risks in school that may cause incidents, injuries and illness, and take the necessary steps to keep everyone as safe as possible. It performs a vital role in protecting everyone from preventable injury, so you would have thought that I would naturally embrace every aspect of its work. However, as a Head I studiously avoided being part of this committee because I had been scarred by my past experience.

In a previous school, when I was young and eager, I had been encouraged to represent the Senior Leadership Team on the governors' health and safety committee. The sitting representative claimed that, 'it would really help my career,' but when I attended my first meeting I quickly discovered that he had passed me a poisoned chalice. While I was grateful for the time and effort the governors put into this committee, their meetings were seriously overcooked. The minimum required from the committee members was a vague interest in matters of health and safety, along with the capacity to attend eight meetings a year. What we actually got was way beyond the maximum safe limit.

These committee members had an intense and boundless enthusiasm for all aspects of health and safety, as well as unlimited time on their hands. For them, the meeting was an afternoon to look forward to. They would greet each other like old friends, they had their own in-jokes, and boy, did they love an anecdote or two, or even twenty-two. No one was more passionate about the minutiae of health and safety than the Chair, Mr Saunders, a retired quantity surveyor, who was never happier than when bogged down in ultra-fine detail.

The result of this was that the meetings were interminable – one of them lasted four hours and thirty-two minutes. I know this because after the first two hours, seen by the committee as a gentle warm-up, I glanced at my watch every five minutes willing it to end.

Every meeting I desperately hoped for something, anything, to change the relentless monotony. Then, during one meeting, a couple of hours into a heated debate about window locks, my prayers were answered. There was a set of windows behind the Chairman's seat that looked out onto the front field. The field led gently down to some flower beds that shielded the school from a busy main road.

Suddenly, a figure shambled into view from the left, skirting the edge of the flower beds. I recognized this person as a local homeless lady from the park over the road who would, on occasion, wander harmlessly onto our site. I thought that maybe she was looking for somewhere to sleep away from the road. No one else in the room had noticed her as they had become quite animated by a proposal for an on-site one-way system. Suddenly, without ceremony, the lady squatted down, hoisted up her skirt, and defecated into one of the flower beds, producing the most enormous stool I had ever seen. Once her business was concluded, she casually rearranged herself and shuffled off out of view, leaving her deposit next to the begonias. It was all I could do not to burst out laughing, and I was just about to interrupt the proceedings to share the news with the committee members, when I managed to stop myself. Of all the people in the world, these were not the ones to tell.

This would be a golden opportunity for them to invoke the Critical Incident Plan. There would be a full investigation and questions would be asked about site access, security camera angles, response times and harmful bacteria. I could see myself being directed to construct a stool-patrol rota and a disinfecting regime. At the very least, it was certain to extend the current meeting considerably, so in the end I decided it would be best to keep the information to myself. However, that little incident did much to sustain me when things got tough in future meetings. If I felt myself beginning to flag, I would stare out the window and smile to myself. I'm not sure whether it was a one-off incident or something more frequent, because I swear the flowers in that flower bed grew better than those in the other beds.

The torturous experience of sitting on this committee had done much to dampen my enthusiasm for health and safety, but this was not the only reason for my lukewarm relationship with what was, after all, a rather significant element of my role. I also had a philosophical objection to the constant drive to reduce risk. I believe that while we have a duty to keep students safe, if we deny students the opportunities to get hurt physically (and indeed emotionally), we are setting them up for failure later in life and helping to create the so-called cotton wool generation. Obviously, I am not encouraging them to have accidents, injuries or any unnecessary trauma – not least because I would inevitably be held responsible – but they do need to be prepared for these as a part of life. Exposing children to some degree of hazard allows them opportunities that encourage self-care skills and autonomous decision-making. In my opinion activities as basic as climbing trees, swinging on ropes, throwing snowballs, playing dodgeball, taking part in a sack race should not be over-regulated or, worse still, banned, as they force students to assess risk, a crucial skill in today's world.

I realized recently how risk-averse a society we have become when I saw a picture of what is believed to be the world's first set of playground swings at Wicksteed Park in Kettering, Northamptonshire, in 1923. The swings bear no resemblance at all to the short, sterile, moulded plastic versions of today. These swings easily look six to seven metres tall, enabling children to swing to crazy heights above the ground with no safety features at all. I am sure they must have caused numerous injuries, but at least the users who ended up with broken limbs and extensive bruising would have been better able to judge risk as they moved on into adulthood.

One of our Year Ten students discovered just how powerful this risk-taking, trial-and-error type of learning can be. She had been happily sitting in her form room one lunchtime when she glanced down at the side of the chair. She noticed that a plastic plug that normally blocked the end of the seat support tube was missing, leaving an open hole. In keeping with the ethos of investigation and exploration that we encourage, she thought: I wonder what will happen if I stick my finger in here. We tried everything – butter, oil, ice – but in the end, we had to hacksaw the main part of the chair off and send her to hospital to have the remaining part removed. The result was she had learned never to do that again.

I experienced something similar myself when I was at school. For a dare, I tightroped across a bar that was fixed over the central well at the top of our main staircase, some five floors up. After my successful attempt, notwithstanding the temporary exclusion I was given, I assessed the risk of such an activity to be low. That was until the bar broke in two when they took it down. It had rusted through after sitting dormant for over a hundred years. Utilizing this as a learning opportunity, I rapidly recalibrated my internal risk assessment and I have never tightroped across a stairwell since, proving that exposure to this sort of risk is good for you.

DECEMBER 2008:
BLOW YOUR OWN HORN

The Year Seven concert takes place in the autumn term and is necessarily a mixture of pleasure and pain. As well as each form group singing their own song together, there is a selection of individual and ensemble pieces. The music teacher holds auditions several weeks before the event, and supply always far outstrips demand. Any student who has ever sung, whistled, held a recorder or seen a piano puts themselves forward to be an act on the night. The music teacher's unenviable task is to pick a blend of acts that represents both the talented and the eager. Sometimes it's hard to find girls that fulfil both criteria, and this is where the pain is generated. I don't think it would be controversial to say that not all of the students who get to perform on the night are gifted musicians or singers.

It was during one concert that I got to witness the very best of our students. The music teacher had been particularly looking forward to the performance of Annabel Stubbs, who played the French horn. She was a shy girl with protective parents, and it had taken a lot of persuasion to get her to perform. However, as the school had not had a horn player in many years, the music teacher was thrilled she had finally agreed. He felt the addition of a French horn added a touch of class to a programme dominated by solo-singing Britney Spears and Katy Perry wannabes. Everything was set up for a virtuoso performance, apart from Annabel's lips. The French horn is a notoriously difficult instrument to play, and it's crucial that its player warms up their lips prior to playing. In her nervousness, Annabel had not warmed up sufficiently, leaving her lips stiff and inflexible – a status at odds with the tuneful mastery of the French horn.

There is usually a zone of tolerance in such musical situations, where a few notes off-key at the beginning of a piece are deemed acceptable. Initially, the audience of girls and Year Seven parents listened politely to these early flaws, but the more it went on, the clearer it became that this was more than just a few dodgy first notes. Annabel, who could hear her own discordant sound, tensed up even further, making her longer notes painful on the ears. People in the audience began glancing at each other. They looked towards the music teacher, to see if his reaction indicated anything was amiss. He, however, had fixed a benign smile on his face. The audience began to get restless, and people started whispering to each other.

'Is the French horn supposed to sound like that?'

'Does that sound out of tune to you?'

The painful performance continued, and the audience began to shift and fidget in their seats. Annabel, caught in the spotlight, was dying a death, and after a particularly long, lingering, tuneless note, she caved. She dropped the horn to her side and, with tears in her eyes, fled the stage.

Her peers might have found this highly amusing, and her exit could well have been accompanied by jeers and laughter. It could have been the amusing story trending at school the next day. Instead, the awkwardness of this situation was short-lived because a group of her classmates took it upon themselves to follow her out. They calmed her down and, after a few minutes' delay, persuaded her to come back out. They escorted her back onto the stage and remained standing on either side of her to provide her with their moral and physical support.

With this protective envelope around her, Annabel managed to pick up where she left off, and to complete the rest of the piece – albeit still off-key.

When she had finished there was a short silence before the girls in her form led the clapping, cheering and thunderous applause for her effort. In fact, she got more applause than if she had merely been an excellent horn player. Some girls even started whooping, although no one went quite so far as to call for an encore. Annabel was taken aback; smiling through her tears, she gave a little bow and then ran straight off the stage again, but this time into the welcoming arms of her parents.

I subsequently watched Annabel's progress up through the school with interest. I was pleased to note that she seemed to suffer no ill-effects from the incident, as she went on to perform for us on many occasions in the future. It is possible that without the kindness of her classmates, she might have been too traumatized by the experience to perform in public again. I knew from the Head of Year that there had been quite a few friendship issues in Annabel's form, with students constantly falling out with each other, but on this occasion, they had rallied around their classmate in a real show of compassion. Their actions undoubtedly boosted Annabel's confidence going forward, so that by the time she left us, she felt confident enough to pursue a career in journalism.

These small acts of kindness can really make a difference and I had experienced something similar earlier in September when I took on the role as Chair of the local Association of Headteachers. It had been at the final meeting the previous year that I had discovered, to my horror, that the Chair of the group was rotated alphabetically, and that in the coming academic year it was my turn. The group met monthly and was made up of all the local secondary heads, frequently supplemented by local authority representatives and invited speakers. It could be a feisty affair, and discussions over funding, admissions and lack of local services often became heated. Having only just completed my first year as a headteacher, the prospect of refereeing some of these gnarled old heads was a daunting one, and I became increasingly nervous as my first meeting as Chair approached.

Fortunately, I had prepared well by making copious notes, putting together a PowerPoint slide show, and walking through each of the agenda items in my mind. Unfortunately, I left my notes behind, and for some reason my PowerPoint wouldn't load, so I was sweaty and apprehensive even before I called the meeting to order. However, I think the other heads must have identified with my predicament because there was an uncharacteristic outbreak of kindness.

Someone lent me their agenda, and the most intimidating of the long-standing heads came over and sorted out the PowerPoint for me. They were considerably politer than usual, talked over each other far less and, on the few occasions I lost my way, gently nudged me back on track. Before they left, several of them made a point of thanking me for chairing. This may not seem like very much, but it meant an awful lot to me. It meant I was no longer afraid of the next meeting, because clearly these established heads were granting me a degree of tolerance until I grew into the role. Kindness is a powerful thing.

A few weeks later, I mentioned to one of the heads how much I had appreciated their forbearance, and he told me of a time where he himself had been the recipient of some real kindness. It was at the start of his very first teaching job where, to look the part, he had used the last of his student grant to buy a suit. Unfortunately, on the first day he was late, and while rushing to morning briefing, he caught his sleeve on a rogue nail in a doorframe. It virtually ripped the arm off the jacket and was such a dramatic tear that he became the centre of attention in the staffroom.

The next day, when he rather disconsolately turned up wearing just the suit trousers and a shirt and tie, he received a visit from the Headteacher. The Head, having seen his predicament at briefing the day before, had gone to town after school and bought him a brand-new suit. A brand-new suit, for goodness' sake! Wow, I thought to myself, what sort of head does that? The kind of head who is thoughtful and generous, and the kind who, as a result of such an action, will inspire lasting loyalty in their colleagues.

Although I never bought anyone a suit, I did make a big effort to thank people as often as I could remember to. Nothing fancy: emails, little cards, biscuits and chocolates for people who had gone over and above or were having a difficult time. The feeling of giving a gift or being kind to someone is similar to the feeling experienced by those receiving it, so kindness really is a win-win situation, and we encourage our students to practise it as much as possible.

JUNE 2009:
THE EMERGENCY NUMBER

While paperwork is the bind for teachers running trips, the bind for a headteacher is that the emergency telephone number is usually yours. If there is an emergency, and sometimes even when there isn't, staff or students will ring you. This means that at a drop of a hat you can be called, often out of hours, during a birthday party, a holiday or an afternoon snooze to remotely manage tricky situations.

One such incident began on an otherwise unremarkable Friday afternoon this summer when I received a hysterical phone call from a girl called Darcy Blunt who was on our Paris trip. During some scheduled 'free time for retail therapy' away from the teachers, her friend Ruth had walked out into the road and been knocked down by a bus in the centre of Paris.

'Is that Dr Smith? Oh, thank God. It's Darcy Blunt. I'm in Paris and Ruth Adams has just been hit by a bus and she looks really bad, and I can't get hold of any of the teachers,' she managed to blurt out before beginning to sob uncontrollably.

It took a good five minutes for me to calm her down and extract the key details from her. It transpired that Ruth had been fiddling with the purchases in her bags when she had stepped out from behind a parked van and into the path of an oncoming bus. Mercifully the bus was decelerating, and the driver managed to slam on the brakes and swerve so that Ruth took a glancing blow and was knocked back towards the pavement. She had lain unconscious for several minutes, having sustained a head injury and damage to her leg. The driver and passers-by had gathered round to help. Someone had called an ambulance, which had arrived within minutes and whisked Ruth off to hospital, leaving Darcy alone by the side of the road. Unfortunately, she did not know her location other than several roads away from 'the really big road' (Champs-Élysées); she did not speak French, she did not know which hospital Ruth had been taken to, and she could not get hold of any of the trip leaders on the phone. She had correctly concluded that now would be a good time to ring the emergency number, and it was at this point that I found myself entering the emergency response phase, which I have named the 'trip tunnel', after the Brussels-coined term for intensified Brexit negotiations.

This tunnel consists of a repeating cycle of frenetic bursts of communication followed by long, anxious intervals waiting for news. The incident was problematic for a number of reasons. Initially I couldn't get hold of any of the staff because their strategy during the shopping trip was to set up camp in a café half way down the Champs-Élysées. This was something I knew they rather enjoyed as it gave them some student-free time in an otherwise hectic schedule. The students were given two hours to roam free in pairs, safe in the knowledge that if there were any problems, they could contact the staff by mobile or come and find them at the café. However, an untimely presidential visit from Barack Obama and his family was not only adding to Paris's famous traffic congestion but was also interfering with the mobile communications in the city centre, so that nobody could get hold of the trip staff.

Back at school we had quickly turned the front office into an impromptu incident room, and I enlisted the help of the other deputy and one of our French teachers. By ringing round all the major Paris hospitals, the French teacher managed to locate Ruth and luckily, even though Darcy and Ruth had ended up on a side road, a long way from the café, Darcy's mobile line held long enough for us to direct her back onto the Champs-Élysées.

I eventually got through by landline to a member of staff who had remained at the hotel, only to find that he had just heard that the coach driver was stuck in gridlock several miles from the shopping trip pick-up point. Just as it looked like things were going pear-shaped, we managed to get through to the café landline and I was able to speak to the trip leader. We agreed that one member of staff, Mrs Knott, would immediately head over to find Ruth in the hospital while the remainder would walk the other students, who had been tearfully reunited with Darcy, across the city to an alternative pick-up point.

It was a long tense afternoon co-ordinating the action between the staff, the hotel, the hospital and the coach driver, as well as reassuring the many worried parents whose calls were beginning to flood in. Eventually, we were able to get the main party onto the coach and back to their hotel on the outskirts of Paris, and Mrs Knott over to Ruth in the hospital. Unfortunately for Ruth and Mrs Knott, there was some further trauma to endure when a fight broke out between some injured pro- and anti-Obama protesters in A&E. They had to cower in their cubicle for a good twenty minutes before order was restored.

Luckily, although Ruth had a broken leg and severe bruising to her head, it was nothing that was permanent or life threatening. When she returned home with Mrs Knott several days after the others, she seemed mainly concerned that she had missed out on a day at Disneyland Paris. I breathed a sigh of relief, confident she was going to make a full recovery. Being in the trip tunnel that afternoon was certainly far more stressful than the Year Nine lesson on food chains I had planned. It meant that for the rest of the year, whenever there was a trip on, I was like a coiled spring nervously waiting for the phone to ring.

NOVEMBER 2010:
HOUR OF NEED

Complying with the old adage, 'you are only as good as the people you surround yourself with', I was keen to surround myself with outstanding senior leaders. Before climbing the management ladder, I had mistakenly believed that this would simply involve appointing people identical to me. I quickly discovered that although it is vital to appoint people with a similar educational philosophy, it is helpful if they are not like you in terms of skills, personalities and behaviours.

Apart from the self-evident truth that having more than one of me on the team would be unbearable, there was plenty of research that suggested that most successful teams are made up of a range of behaviour and personality types. I had already also learnt from observing previous headteachers that it is important to have deputies who can cover your inadequacies, so it was jolly lucky that Mr Gregory, Mr Charlwood and I were all very different.

Mr Gregory was a creative, free-thinking, people-orientated person, while Mr Charlwood was a meticulous implementer with formidable attention to detail. A simple example of how different we were was evident in our differing approach to desktop etiquette. I am unable to work with any extraneous items scattered about, as a cluttered desktop confuses my mind and muddles my thinking. Mr Gregory on the other hand was a borderline hoarder and tossed everything and anything that came his way onto his desk. It was piled so high with towers of paraphernalia that he disappeared when he sat down, and I could not understand how he functioned efficiently. He called it his 'volcano filing system', because he claimed that if he ever needed a document, it would eventually spew out of the top of one of the piles. Mr Charlwood's desk was somewhere between the two of us, and these two, along with the rest of the team, provided a range of skills and behaviours that prevented me having a myopic view of things. Much like marmite peanut butter or croissant donuts, the whole was greater than the sum of its parts, and having created such a desirable blend of individuals, it was probably in my best interests to listen to them.

One occasion when I didn't, and went on to pay the price, was the 'Big Year Seven Sleepover' – a well-intentioned idea of mine that went horribly wrong. It came about because I thought that the Year Seven students, who came from many different primary schools, could do with a bit more bonding, so I came up with the idea of a sleepover. Everyone else in my team pointed out the obvious flaw in my plan, which is that if you put 120 adolescents in a hall overnight, they won't go to sleep. Mistakenly ignoring these naysayers and doom-mongers, I forged ahead, encouraged by the ecstatic response I received when I advertized the event in a Year Seven assembly. In my mind's eye, proceedings would benignly conclude around 11 p.m., when they tucked down into their sleeping bags with a hot chocolate, tired but happy.

I knew things had gone awry when, at 9 p.m. on the evening of the sleepover, I arrived back at school from another event. The corridors were strewn with rubbish, students were running around screaming, two girls were crying in a corner and there was very loud dance music emanating from the hall.

I was met by Mr Charlwood, who had just compèred the quiz; he had wild eyes, a hoarse voice and a shirt drenched in sweat.

Shell-shocked, he told me that the evening hadn't gone to plan because the students had consumed unfeasibly large quantities of additive-laden sweets with energy drinks. This meant the subsequent quiz had been manic. They had not listened to the questions; they had shouted out the answers and rival teams had fallen out, so he had gone straight into a video dance game in an attempt to dissipate their energy. This had not worked either; they remained hyperactive, and within twenty minutes even more of them had fallen out and several tearful girls had called their parents asking them to take them home. It was rapidly turning into a disaster so, as an aspiring Hero Head, I waded in, turned off the dance video, and told them we were going over to the sports hall early, to watch a film.

My vision of them going to sleep at 11 p.m. proved to be ridiculous for several reasons:

* They did not want to.
* They had high levels of caffeine and additives in their blood.
* The hall was cold and the floor was hard and uncomfortable.

Instead, they whispered excitedly to each other and, because there were so many of them spread out across the hall in clumps of sleeping bags, when the lights were off it was difficult to identify who was talking. As we patrolled, they would stop talking when we came near and then continue once we had gone past. It turned into a war of attrition and our threats became increasingly vicious. It was 2:30 a.m. before a semblance of quiet broke out and I could finally retire upstairs to sleep in the PE teaching room.

This was problematic because it had come to light earlier that one of the girls didn't have a sleeping bag. When she told me this I had considered, probably for longer than was morally reasonable, extolling the virtues of a bed fashioned from a coat, but I knew deep down there was only one honourable thing to do. She seemed quite taken with my top-of-the-range, season-four-rated duck-down bag with draft collar and insulated zip baffles.

I, however, was now left to fashion my own bed out of my coat and realized there was no virtue in such a construction whatsoever. Not only that, but if I moved, I triggered a sensor that turned on the landing lights and bathed the hall in light. After two hours on a cold, hard floor, with only my coat for comfort, and unable to move an inch for fear of triggering the lights, I finally drifted off to the sound of someone sobbing down below. Twenty minutes later I was woken because the sobbing girl's mum had arrived to take her home and, as it was 5 a.m. at this point, I decided I might as well get up.

In the end, the 'Big Year Seven Sleepover' was in fact a

misnomer and was referred to from then on as the 'Big Year Seven Wakeover'. I couldn't really moan about it because firstly, it had been my idea, and secondly, the rest of the staff on duty had to take these sleep-deprived and fractious Year Sevens straight to a theme park the next morning for a bit more bonding. The next week I received the following letter:

Dear Dr Smith,

I would like to thank you for lending me your sleeping bag at the Big Sleepover. I am extremely grateful for your kindness. I wanted to express my gratitude by doing a letter. Also thank you for directing me to my class when I was lost. You may not remember it, but I do because you were there in my hour of need. I hope every student is able to talk to you because you are a fabulous headmaster.

Sincerely,
Isabelle Galloway

What a perceptive young girl! I had a feeling she would go far. However, the real lesson I learnt from the whole fiasco was that if you are going to take the trouble of assembling a diverse and multi-talented team, then it might be wise to listen to them, especially when they are unanimously against your latest bright idea.

JANUARY 2011:
AUSTERITY

The year spanning 2010 to 2011 coincided with my third year of headship. It was also the beginning of austerity measures in the UK. If only I had known what a financial bonanza the previous three years had been compared to what was to come, then I would have revelled in all the lovely wonga. If we were presently funded at the same rate as we were back then in 2010, we would receive over three-quarters of a million pounds more in our yearly budget!

As we managed to endure the years of austerity and still maintain academic standards, the government may well have concluded that the system must have been bloated all along. However, because the regime during this period judged us principally on results, we preferentially protected activities related to exam performance while slashing other important and enriching activities. We were forced to make material changes that had a significant effect on our students. For example, we couldn't buy any of the latest textbooks, so our students were often studying from books that did not cover the full course content. The roof of our eighty-year-old building leaked, so we regularly had to put buckets in the corridors and classrooms to catch the water that trickled from the waterlogged ceilings every time it rained. Pressures on the local authority budget meant that the in-school health provision was massively scaled back, including the termination of our weekly in-school sexual health clinic. When I first arrived in Torbay it had the highest rate of teenage pregnancies in the UK, and I was asked to represent the secondary schools on the council committee trying to reverse this trend. Even after my time on the committee I followed with interest the positive progress they had made in this area. A decision like this, to slash an oversubscribed clinic of this nature, was a significant indicator to me of just how desperate things had become.

We axed subjects like design and technology, as we did not have the money to staff the smaller numbers wanting to do them, just at the time when schools were being accused of not doing enough to encourage girls into this sort of area. I found myself repeatedly having to ask parents to donate money for various projects – nothing fancy, just replacement computers, minibuses and sports equipment, the sort of things you would expect a school to have. Some of the parents could not afford to donate and others rightly believed they had already paid for a state education through their taxes. As a beneficiary and supporter of state education, this was not quite what I had envisioned myself doing when I became a headteacher. However, the awkwardness of asking for money was nothing compared to the challenges my teachers experienced during austerity. The true cost of the cuts fell on them.

They ended up with more teaching groups, more contact time and larger class sizes. Don't let anyone tell you that larger class sizes have no effect on outcomes. An A-level chemistry class of thirty-two is a completely different beast to one of twelve, not least in terms of the limited individual feedback you can provide, or the epic effort required to stage a class practical. Despite the debate about the degree of benefit smaller class sizes have on student outcomes, to my mind there is no debate about the detrimental effect larger class sizes have on teacher outcomes. Larger classes clearly cause an increase in teacher workload, with a consequent reduction in teacher wellbeing.

Teachers absorbed this increased demand because they are altruistic, they genuinely want to help their students and, when push came to shove, they dipped into the well of goodwill to ensure their students were not affected, but this challenge caused considerable wear and tear, and not all of them made it through. Prolonged exposure to this sort of pressure can, all too often, cause good people to leave the profession. The well of goodwill is now bone dry, so if you, like that great educationalist Whitney Houston, believe the children are our future, I implore you to canvass anyone and everyone in any appropriate forum to promote more funding for education.

At one point, this lack of funding drove five local headteachers and I to take a day out of school to travel to Parliament (a 474-mile round trip) for a meeting with the schools minister. There was a tug of war between us and the local authority over some funding, and as the final decision was his, we went up to make our case. It was a very amiable and positive meeting. It was only when we got back home that we discovered that at precisely the moment we were sat in a parliamentary committee room, hobnobbing with the minister, one of his minions had sent an email to our local authority awarding them the money. They had already made the decision before we met! Our objective had been to get more money for our schools, but our efforts collectively cost our schools over £2,500 in train tickets, tube fares and salaries on a pointless visit.

I could go on and on about how these cuts make it hard to provide a more holistic education for our students, and I often do. The main person I go on and on to is my wife, Caroline. This is despite the fact that she had very kindly looked in her purse several times to see if she could bail us out, only to discover that she was several hundreds of thousands of pounds short of what we required. However, it is a very necessary part of the de-stressing process for teachers to go home and moan about their day/students/colleagues/school to their partners. I have been doing it for years, but while I had ended up looking after able secondary school girls, Caroline had become the manager of a regional unit for primary school children with autism. This meant that if I began moaning about difficulties such as the underfunding we were experiencing, she could instantly trump it by describing a day that may, for example, have involved a runaway child, angry parents, the police, social services, smeared excrement and teeth marks on her arm. This would usually stimulate a period of quiet contemplation on my part, after which my situation did not seem quite so bad after all.

APRIL 2011:
IT'S A JUNGLE OUT THERE

One consequence of the financial challenge facing schools was a seismic shift in the importance of student recruitment. Prior to this we nonchalantly filled up our Year Seven places and the vast majority of the Year Eleven students would drift into our sixth form without a second thought. This all changed during austerity because the only way for schools to generate more income was to retain their own students and then go out and steal someone else's. This meant that students were bombarded by charm offensives from competing schools and colleges.

I found that more and more of my time was taken up with recruitment-related activities such as producing a glossy prospectus, purchasing pop-up banners and commissioning promotional videos. We put on weekly tours and extra all-singing-and-dancing open evenings. We gave out school badges like confetti and offered potential sixth formers personal tablets, free gym membership and everything short of guaranteeing them three A* grades at A-level, although I was tempted to offer this as an 'early bird' incentive.

This is not what the public purse should be used for, but schools had their financial backs to the wall and there was little choice but to use all means available to survive in the new recruitment jungle.

There were two main weaknesses in our corporate offer. The first was that our main building was tired and worn after eight decades of teenage use, and the other was that we didn't have any boys. The latter was easily addressed because, fortuitously, there were 1,200 of them only 500 yards away at the adjacent boys' grammar school. Generations of our girls had become adept, even ingenious, at getting to meet with them, and the issue was one of too much contact, not too little. The building issue was more difficult to gloss over.

One parent, on an open day, listened to all the wonderful things we did for our students but insisted on droning on about the poor appearance of the main building. In the end, I snapped and recommended that he visit another school down the road with a shiny new £26-million building. He began to drool as I outlined its wide, damp-free corridors, light and airy atrium and extensive sports facilities. I encouraged him to arrange a visit first thing next morning and, as I got the impression that he didn't want minor considerations such as curriculum, achievement or pastoral care to cloud his judgement, I didn't bother to tell him that Ofsted had deemed that it required improvement.

There was a rather unfortunate end to one of my school tours in the summer. Despite my best efforts, one couple looked sceptical about my ability to provide the right environment for their daughter, so, to further extol the virtues of our school, I accompanied them to the front entrance. While I was talking, something behind me caught their attention at about the same time as a strong and unmistakable smell of cannabis wafted over us. The couple looked at each other, abruptly concluded the conversation and quick-marched out of the main entrance.

I spun round to identify what had caught their attention, only to find a cluster of condoms lying on the grass verge behind me. They were the innocent residue of Year Eleven's last-day shenanigans when they had been blown up to decorate our school sign. The cannabis cloud came courtesy of a neighbour who used the shed at the end of his garden for relaxation purposes, and he had chosen that moment to partake of some weed. Such was the pressure to recruit that I considered scooping up the condoms and chasing after the couple to prove they were unused, and I probably would have if they had not disappeared from view. For consolation, I moved closer to our neighbour's shed, took several deep breaths and felt a whole lot more relaxed about losing the sale.

Ideally schools should focus on doing what is best for their own students without having to compare or compete with others. However, the educational environment is now inherently competitive. A key policy of David Cameron's coalition government was to drive up standards through competition. The consequent need for schools to compete for students and funding, in addition to the pressure of league tables and Ofsted ratings, has meant that other schools can be regarded as competitors rather than colleagues. This marketized approach is a real challenge to collaborative school relationships.

I once came across an interesting model of how these competitive relationships might function. In broad terms the model categorized schools into one of only two types: they could either be great, or they could be crap, and this resulted in the following four types of inter-school relationship:

1 We're great; you're great.
2 We're great; you're crap.
3 We're crap; you're great.
4 We're crap; you're crap.

At various times, in various schools, I have experienced all four of these relationships. The 'we're great; you're great' type was an uneasy relationship. We grudgingly acknowledged that the other school was great, but we secretly believed ourselves to be greater, and they believed the same of themselves. Consequently, although the relationship was cordial and respectful, we avoided sharing any resources or advice that might give them the edge over us and vice versa.

When I was in a school where we thought we were great, and we perceived the other school to be crap, their mere existence validated our excellence. So we lorded it over them, happy to throw them a few helpful scraps from our fully laden advice table, as long as they stayed in their place and did not improve too much.

When I was in a crap school and the other school was great, we moaned incessantly about all the perceived advantages and benefits they had over us. We refused to copy any of their methods or systems because we churlishly clung on to the idea that, 'that wouldn't work here'. We constantly repeated the mantra, 'they may do better than us but we really care about our students'. Obviously, we didn't care enough about our students to get them better exam results.

The best school-to-school relationship I experienced was when our school was crap and so was the other school. The staff from the two schools got on famously. Together, we wallowed in the mire and generously shared a whole load of crappy systems and resources, along with a healthy dose of gallows humour.

Of course, schools are not completely great or completely crap, so the model is flawed. The truth is, it is very difficult to compare schools fairly because their circumstances can be very different; not that this stops anyone from doing it. If the government really wants schools to form lasting effective collaborations for the improvement of all schools, then they need to change the competitive culture that has created this fragmentation and isolation.

They may want to take note of the fact that in 2013 the OECD found no evidence, from its international analysis, that competition between private, state, charter-style schools in the US, or free schools in the UK, had any impact on raising standards. Andreas Schleicher, the OECD's Deputy Director at the time said, 'You might expect systems with greater choice would do better, because competition would put out of the market schools that did not succeed; but the evidence showed no such correlation.' In fact, the celebrated competitive Swedish free school movement, which partly inspired the UK government's own free schools, was branded a political failure by its own education minister in 2012, when the performance of its schools showed the steepest decline of any OECD country.

Schleicher said, 'Competition alone is not a predictor for better outcomes and the UK is a good example of this: a highly competitive school system but still only an average performer.' He went on to say that the success of education systems such as Shanghai's was the result of an emphasis on teacher selection, as well as prioritizing investment in teacher training and development.

A very significant adverse effect of austerity was my inability to invest in teacher development – one of the key methods of improving a school. It was all getting very frustrating.

JULY 2011:
HOW THEY CHANGE

At the end of the summer term every year, the school has a sponsored walk to raise money for charity. This involves the whole school, staff and students, walking down to the pier at Torquay harbour and boarding a flotilla of local ferries. These race across the bay to Brixham, where their human cargo spills onto the harbour arm. Here the girls pause to tighten the straps of their backpacks, tie any loose shoelaces and swig from their drinks bottles before hiking the ten miles back to school along the coast path.

The walk has a carnival-like atmosphere with many of the girls wearing fancy dress. Along the way they register at various checkpoints and stop from time to time to rest their legs, eat their packed lunches or refuel from the beachside food outlets at Broadsands, Goodrington and Paignton. As they walk at different speeds, the six hundred or so participants soon get strung out in groups along the route, each moving at its own pace. Right at the front of the pack, led by the indefatigable Mrs Payne, our Head of PE, are some of the older girls who run all the way.

Right at the back of the pack is me, the sweeper. My role is to walk behind the stragglers, sweeping up any students that fall behind the timeline that would get them back to school before the final bell. It's a thankless task; I have to walk behind those students who generally regard plodding to the kitchen and back as a bit of a hike. I can cope with those who have absolutely no hope of making it, because I simply call the 'mop-up minibus' we have on standby to pick them up and drive them back to school. Far more painful are those who walk at an inconceivably slow pace but will probably just about make it back in time if I repeatedly prod them with a pointy stick and the wind stays in the right direction. Walking behind these dawdlers means that not only do I have to walk at the speed of a sloth, but I remain within earshot of them as well.

This year the laggards at the back were two Year Eight students, a girl called Sabrina Petersen and her friend, who between them left me with an indelible memory of the sponsored walk. Since I was the sweeper, the need to stay close enough to keep these foot-draggers moving along meant there was no real way of escaping their conversation. Their ramblings covered such weighty topics as: which taste nicer: pink or white marshmallows; when was the last time either of them had stepped in dog mess; and whether, if they had to make a choice, they would choose to have one extra finger or one less. For five interminable hours they produced a continuous stream of surreal speculation that almost finished me off. I lost count of the times I offered to get the mop-up minibus to take them home. I think I even begged them at one point with the promise of a huge number of house points, but as they were quite happy ambling along, they declined. It was a blessed relief when we finally arrived back at school. As they headed off towards the buses in a deep discussion about the best sleeps they'd ever had, I remember thinking that if these were the typical thoughts of the younger generation then the future wellbeing of the nation was in doubt.

It was another five years before I spent any significant amount of time with either of them again. It was during our mock Oxbridge interviews that I came face to face with Sabrina for the first time since the walk. I was intrigued to see she was applying to do Politics at Cambridge and, with painful memories of her Year Eight musings, I was keen to see how she would get on; if I'm honest, I feared the worst. Our mock interview set-up was quite intimidating, with a panel made up of senior teachers, subject experts and a fierce external advisor we brought in every year to spice things up.

Sabrina appeared unfazed by any of this and took to her seat looking strangely calm and confident. Under the intense scrutiny of the panel, I wondered how long it would be before self-doubt set in and this faux confidence ebbed away. When the first question asked was something along the lines of, 'Should a political party define ideology, or should ideology define the party?' I braced myself for an awkward response.

Well, oh me of little faith! It was a good few minutes before Sabrina eloquently drew the compelling strands of her cogent argument to a conclusion and we were able to catch our breath; her depth of knowledge, her impressive logic and her impassioned, masterful delivery simply blew us away. Stunned at her first answer we fired some more difficult questions at her, but there was nothing she could not riposte with ease, and she even seemed to enjoy sparring with the external advisor.

It was one of the most mesmeric mock interviews any of us had witnessed and, in stark contrast to the last time we had met, I was so keen to hear more that we ran way over time. After she had left, we all agreed that she had been a truly exceptional interviewee and would most likely next come to our attention as a member of the cabinet. Sabrina had come a long way since I had listened to her wittering on about marshmallows and best ever sleeps. It turned out I had been needlessly worrying about the future wellbeing of our nation after all. It was a further reminder to me of how important it is that we keep faith in all our young people. If we can guide them through the teething problems of youth, however painful, with encouragement and the provision of the right opportunities, they can flourish.

My time as a teacher has been peppered with examples of students surprising us through how they've developed into promising young adults, and Demi Broome in particular springs to mind.

Demi Broome was a very angry young girl whose behaviour became increasingly difficult as she passed up through the school. In Year Eight she was caught smoking in the changing rooms, and in Year Nine she was found on the Ash Path, a path at the back of the school, with a stash of alco-pops in her bag. In Year Ten she started getting into trouble outside of school by hanging around with a much older crowd, and by Year Eleven this included getting into drunken fights on nights out at the weekend.

Demi was no fool, but this lifestyle was incompatible with her schoolwork. While she did usually make it into school each day, she was often dishevelled, late, tired or hungover. She rarely had the right equipment or had done any of the homework. She was quick to anger and really struggled to concentrate in lessons. The pastoral team were constantly having to calm her down, help her catch up and try to get her back on track.

This daily war gave us the impression that she hated school and couldn't wait to leave – a belief reinforced when, after her last exam in Year Eleven, she decided to burn all her books and notes because, as she put it, 'I aint ever gonna read that shit again.' Unfortunately, this endeavour went horribly wrong because she set light to them on a path by the field, and after the long hot summer, the dried-out scrub along the side of the path caught fire. The fire quickly spread down the slope towards the adjacent primary school. On seeing the billowing smoke and approaching fire, they sounded their fire alarm and evacuated their staff and students from the building, but during the evacuation their Deputy Headteacher fell down the stairs and broke her arm.

This caused considerable upset, and despite my profuse apologies, relations remained frosty between our two schools for several years after that. It seemed that Demi's time at school was ending in a manner that typified her five years with us. After giving her a final severe reprimand there was a sense of a relief when she left my office for the last time. As I watched her storm off down the driveway, I thought that she was probably glad to see the back of us, too.

It came as some surprise, therefore, when towards the end of the autumn term, I saw her back in the foyer. Wary as to why she had come in, and hoping it was not the sign of yet more trouble, I gave her a rather guarded welcome and asked what she was after. With a rare smile she said she had come in to tell us her news. She explained that she had managed to sort out some of the issues in her life and went on to proudly tell us that she had got herself a job as a nursing ancillary and was loving every minute of it. She had wanted to come back in to personally thank the pastoral staff who had put up with her over the years and had helped her to achieve a good set of GCSE results.

During the conversation, I was amazed to discover that she really missed being at school, and despite all of the conflict she had generated she looked back on her schooldays with fondness. She said it had been the only stable part of her life and the place she felt most secure. This revelation was a salient reminder to me of the role schools can play in the lives of students whose experiences outside of school are challenging.

The thing that Demi most needed from us was not a string of top grades, but to know that someone cared about how she was and wanted to help her even if she didn't always accept that help. I took her down to see her pastoral team for what turned out to be a surprisingly joyous reunion. A few years later I was further heartened to hear that Demi was training to become a nurse.

JULY 2012:
CATERING FOR THE MASSES

With a thousand hungry students on-site, providing a continuous supply of nutritious food is an absolute necessity. However, in every single school I have worked in, there have been more complaints from the students about the food than there have been about all the other issues combined, with uniform and toilets coming a distant second and third. It is almost impossible to please all of the students all of the time. They will complain that the food is too expensive, too fatty, too many carbs, not enough carbs, the portions are too small, too big, too much mayonnaise, not enough mayonnaise, not enough options, etc. It is no easy task for the kitchen staff to cater for the needs of the masses, so they could do without any distractions.

One such distraction came this month when the kitchen manager rang asking me to come down to the kitchen. The kitchen staff thought they had caught one of our Year Nine students stealing. They had her detained in the kitchen office, but the girl was refusing to empty her pockets. When I arrived, I discovered their captive was a sullen-looking Year Nine girl called Rebecca Leah, whom I immediately escorted back to her Head of Year's office for interrogation. I asked her to empty her pockets and, after a brief show of resistance, she removed a chocolate brownie wrapped in plastic and slammed it down on the desk in front of us. For a brief moment all three of us stared at the offending article.

The brownie represented very different things to each of us. To me it represented a deviation from the values we were hoping to nurture in our students. Stealing was dishonest, a betrayal of trust. I began to gather in my mind the hackneyed phrases I would reprimand her with: 'We are very disappointed in you'; 'You have let us, your family, but most of all, yourself down'; 'Stealing is not big and it's not clever'; etc. I readied myself to go through the motions.

Luckily, Mrs Mellor, her Head of Year, was a wise old owl with many years of pastoral experience, and to her the stolen chocolate brownie represented something very different. It was a warning sign, an alert. All was not well here, and this theft was a symptom of something deeper going on in Leah's life. She quickly pre-empted my impending crassness by asking Leah how her mother was.

This was all it took for Leah to crumble, and her initial surliness quickly evaporated to be replaced by weeping. Her mother, a single parent, had poor mental health. Because of this, Leah's family life was chaotic and disorganized, and although most of the time she and her younger brother were able to navigate a way through it, there were episodes when her mother's illness was more significant, and she was unable to look after them properly. This might manifest itself in her not coming out of her room for days on end or, as was the case on this occasion, by impulsively blowing all their benefit money on something frivolous, leaving none with which to buy food.

Although Leah was entitled to a free school meal, this was all she and her brother were going to get that day because there were still another three days until their mother's next benefit payment. To Leah, the chocolate brownie represented the difference between her and her brother having something to eat that evening or going hungry. I thanked my lucky stars that we had people like Mrs Mellor on the team – people who made it their business to know what was going on in the lives of our students.

I made a token gesture of pointing out to Leah that stealing was not the way forward. I put much more emphasis on making it clear that if she found herself in a similar situation in the future, she had to let us know. Our focus then shifted to re-engaging the social and mental health teams with Leah's mother, which unfortunately was not an insubstantial task given that, like us, their services had been cut to the bone during austerity. After school,

Mrs Mellor drove Leah and her brother home via the supermarket, where she used some of our emergency fund to purchase enough food to tide the family over until their benefit money arrived.

Our main fear going forward was the upcoming summer holiday, when Leah and her brother would no longer be able to access a free school meal. The provision of free school meals has many benefits. Research by the Institute for Fiscal Studies has shown that the provision of universal infant free school meals during term time boosted attainment in disadvantaged local authorities. But other arguments for providing them during term time, like the provision of a balanced nutritious meal and the creation of an environment in which children from low-income families feel valued, continue to apply during the school holidays as well. The obvious stumbling block for providing free meals in the holidays is the cost, but as we are one of the world's richest nations, surely not letting any of our children go hungry should be a national priority. Clearly not. It was another eight years before a modern-day saint, in the form of the footballer Marcus Rashford, shamed the government into providing food vouchers for low-income families during the summer holidays.

In the meantime, from our outdoor education store, I dug out some of the leftover dehydrated meal sachets that our students use on their camping expeditions. I gave them to Leah and told her to stash them away in case of a future emergency.

MAY 2013:
THE TEN TORS

The Ten Tors is the pre-eminent walking challenge for young people in Britain. The event has been running since 1960 and typically involves around 2,400 teenagers in 400 teams of six. Teams navigate 35, 45 or 55 miles over Dartmoor National Park to visit ten nominated granite outcrops called tors. They must do this in under two days and must be self-sufficient by carrying all the equipment they need to complete the route and stay out safely overnight.

It is no mean feat, as the rugged, boggy terrain, the long distances and the weather can conspire against the participants. The teams need to start their training months in advance in order to gain the navigation skills, campcraft and fitness levels required to succeed. They are helped in this respect by an army of volunteer leaders, many of whom are weather-beaten old lags who have helped prepare generations of young people for the event. The old lag at our school was Dr Coles, a whippet-thin ex-geography teacher, who was our Head of Outdoor Education. He was an expert in survival techniques; not only could he forage a hearty meal out of the seemingly barren landscape, but he could navigate his way through the treacherous bogs using only his sense of smell. His blister-management skills were of international standard, and he was well versed in the folklore of both Dartmoor and the Ten Tors.

On pitch-black training nights, he would spook our girls with campfire ghost stories and fondly reminisce about the Ten Tors of '96, when driving snow necessitated a mass evacuation of the moors. It was the extensive training our students received from Dr Coles and his loyal band of helpers that maintained the school's enviable reputation in this event.

The event is organized by the Army from their Okehampton Camp, supported by both the Royal Navy and Royal Air Force. The services use it as a logistics training exercise, and among other things they provide the tor-top checkpoints as well as land and air support for those who drop out through injury, exhaustion or exposure to extremes of temperature. For the weekend of the walk the army camp takes on the look of Glastonbury Festival, as between them, the 400 teams erect a bewildering array of tents, marquees and camp kitchens. Food vendors and stallholders stake their pitches alongside rows of portable toilets and, if it's wet, there is mud aplenty.

I usually pop up to Okehampton each year to give our teams a send-off, and this year I escorted one of our 45-mile teams to the start. The nominated team leader was a girl called Amber Eden who, despite being very personable, was yet to register as a student of note on our radar. As I gave her team a few last words of advice and encouragement, little did I know that she was about to write herself into our school's Ten Tors history.

The start of the Ten Tors event is one of the seven wonders of the Southwest. High on a ridge just south of Okehampton Army Camp, the thousands of participants, their trainers and well-wishers form an enormous crescent facing the spectacular vista of the northern moor. With army helicopters circling overhead, an expectant hush descends during the traditional reading of the Ten Tors Prayer. This is the prelude to the firing of the field guns that signal the start of the challenge.

The organizers are at pains to stress that the Ten Tors is not a competition between teams, but a challenge between each participant and the course. Most teams completely ignore this and race to be the first to finish on their particular route. The boom of the cannon unleashes a charge like a battle scene from *Lord of the Rings*. Several thousand backpack-laden adolescents, resplendent in their team colours and wildly waving their flags, surge down the hillside to gain an early lead over the other teams. Invariably, someone falls over and turns an ankle or breaks a limb and must suffer the humiliation of being stretchered back past the crowd, even before the last of the teams have disappeared over the horizon. The start is all over in twenty minutes, after which the well-wishers depart until Sunday, when they will return to cheer their teams across the finish line. Meanwhile the trainers return to camp and nervously monitor the progress of their teams on screens in the Army Communications Centre.

As Saturday progressed, fog and mist descended and reduced visibility to as little as ten metres. The accompanying rain added to the already swollen rivers, making the river crossings hazardous. Overnight the temperatures dropped to near freezing, and throughout Sunday the weather worsened further still.

Amber Eden led her team as best she could, given the adverse conditions, but when they were unable to traverse one of the engorged river crossings on their route, they had to detour several miles out of their way to get beyond it. Late on Saturday afternoon, when they were tired, wet and way off course, they came across an inexperienced 35-mile team who were wandering around completely lost after their maps had blown away.

Amber assumed overall charge of both groups and led them all to some higher ground where they pitched their tents and attempted to hunker down for the night. After a sodden and pretty much sleepless night, they arose in the morning to find the weather was no better. Amber knew she had to decide whether to continue. There was a slim chance that if they kept going, they might get back on track and finish the course, but if the weather worsened, they were in danger of becoming stranded and at risk of exposure. As the team leader she had been entrusted with an electronic tracking device which had a red emergency button that could be pushed to call for assistance. As it would trigger a rescue operation from the military and civilian emergency services that could involve the scrambling of helicopters, land vehicles and rescue teams, the decision to activate it was not one to be taken lightly.

Amber agonized over what to do, but as she could see no improvement in the weather, and the rivers and streams around them still appeared to be rising, she proposed that they throw in the towel. This suggestion was met with immediate resistance from the members of both teams. They vehemently argued that they had invested too much time and energy to give up now, and that they would rather take a risk with the weather and keep going. Amber did her utmost to persuade them to change their minds, but they were adamant and, after the debate got quite heated, they called for a vote, which she lost 11:1.

Amber found herself a lone voice, burdened with the choice of either letting the others take a gamble on the conditions improving or preventing both teams from completing the challenge by calling for assistance. It was a tricky dilemma, but it was at this point that Amber Eden stepped out of the shadows and revealed her leadership credentials. Despite the peer pressure, generally agreed by teenagers to be the strongest force known to humankind, she went against all their wishes and pushed the emergency button. This took a considerable amount of self-belief and guts, but she believed it was the right thing to do in the circumstances – if she could not reasonably guarantee their safety, then the goal was not worth the risk. They would be better off retiring unharmed to try again next year.

Understandably, her unilateral action did not go down at all well with her companions. This meant she had to endure an intense period of criticism, followed by several hours of sullen resentment, before they were eventually found by the Army and evacuated from the moor.

When they talked to their Army rescuers, it soon became apparent that the situation was much more serious than they had thought. Weather conditions across the moor had become increasingly extreme, and it would have been virtually impossible for them to complete their route. The 2013 event subsequently went down as one of the most miserable in Ten Tors history, with over five hundred of the participants failing to complete the course. Dr Coles and I praised Amber's courageous decision-making, and her teammates came to appreciate it too, especially when it transpired that one of them had developed hypothermia. It is possible that she may well have saved their lives. This demonstration of leadership from Amber turned out to be no flash in the pan, as three years later she graduated as a naval officer from the Britannia Royal Naval College in Dartmouth. We now use her as an example to encourage our girls to take on leadership roles.

In my mind the Ten Tors Challenge is one of the most valuable activities our students can engage with during their time with us. The mental and physical challenge involved is a life-changing experience for many and they will undoubtedly remember it for the rest of their lives. It also changed my life somewhat because it was while I was helping Dr Coles on some of the training weekends that I got myself hooked on 'tor bagging'.

This is the practice of visiting and touching as many of the granite outcrops in Dartmoor National Park as you can. Over time the elements have shaped many of the tors into weird and wonderful shapes, as well as creating notable features like rock basins and giant boulders that rest on each other, called logan stones. Many tors have curious names like the Bowerman's Nose, Branscombe's Loaf and Figgie Daniel, although my absolute favourite is Little Mis Tor, which I would like to propose as the next Mr Man/Little Miss character.

Although they are inanimate lumps of granite, I have become quite fond of some of the tors, and nowadays when I revisit them it feels like I'm meeting with old friends. Not only did I warm to the task of recording each tor I visited on a spreadsheet, but I also logged other helpful details such as the grid reference, notable features and weather conditions, and for good measure I took a photograph, just to prove I had been there. It wasn't long before I became a nerd possessed and spent every spare waking hour in pursuit of yet more tors. I was guided by a book called *Dartmoor's Tors and Rocks* by Ken Ringwood, a member of the Dartmoor Search and Rescue Team. As his book listed 365 tors, it was quite a task, particularly as many of them were remote.

After nine intense months I finally bagged all 365 tors, and for validation I invited Ken Ringwood himself around for tea. Once he had satisfied himself that I was not a madman, he revealed that he had not actually touched all of the tors but had taken pictures of a couple of them from a distance instead. This admission meant that, as far as we both knew, I was the first person to touch all 365 tors (and rocks) in his book, and he very kindly signed my copy with words to that effect.

I had never been the first to do anything in my life, so to commemorate this feat I did what any self-respecting nerd would do and made an enormous scale model of all 365 tors out of small wooden blocks. This monstrosity now hangs in our school library, but rather than becoming the item of interest I hoped it would, it just seems to have cemented my image as a bit of an odd chap. I get the feeling that the librarians would prefer it if the model were removed, but one of the perks of being a headteacher is that you are in charge, so that model is staying where it is.

DECEMBER 2013:
THE LAW OF UNINTENDED CONSEQUENCES

I believe that most leaders genuinely want to do the best for their staff, and if they can think of ways of improving their working experience, then they will. However, they should beware of the 'law of unintended consequences'. This is where positive actions often have negative effects that are unanticipated or unintended. I have fallen foul of this law on numerous occasions when, despite my good intentions, I ended up upsetting people.

The most notable incident was in the lead-up to Christmas 2013, when I decided to organize a mulled wine social for the support staff. As it was difficult for many of them to attend the staff lunchtime buffet, I thought I would provide an alternative get-together for them at breaktime. What could possibly go wrong?

I really went for it: I decked out a room with Christmas lights; I set up a sound system that blasted out Christmas carols; and I brought a shedload of mulled wine and mince pies. I even dressed up as Santa and personally ladled each of them a glass of hot mulled wine from a steaming urn.

While most people seemed to enjoy themselves, there were some niggles. A few people complained because I was only serving mulled wine. I'd mistakenly thought that the festive card I had sent out inviting them to a mulled wine mingle would have indicated the nature of the event, but this seemed to have passed them by. To placate the protesters, I let them use the small stash of soft drinks I had brought in for the later lunchtime buffet. Another person challenged me on why we were using school funds to pay for staff to drink alcohol. I tried to reassure him that I had actually paid for it myself, but he remained unconvinced and refused to have a drink, though he stayed on to complain to everyone about the misuse of taxpayers' money.

Things got worse at the lunchtime staff buffet. My depleted drinks supply was soon exhausted, leaving no soft drinks for those who arrived later. Despite there being a cold-water drinking dispenser and tea-making facilities in the staffroom next door, it was brought to my attention that we had provided the support staff with mulled wine earlier, but apparently couldn't be bothered to provide the teachers with soft drinks. This discontent spread and spoilt both the atmosphere and the fine spread of food; several groups took their buffet with them to eat in their department areas.

At the end of lunch, I had to rush off to oversee the sixth form Christmas entertainment and I returned to find the cleaning supervisor waiting for me. She wanted to complain about the mess we had left behind and let me know that her team would not do the washing-up, as it was not part of their job. At the end of the day, when students and staff were shouting their cheery yuletide goodbyes, I made a start on the washing-up. Luckily there was an awful lot of it, so I had plenty of time to contemplate the law of unintended consequences.

It is incredible how well-intentioned actions can generate discord. One year, when I felt staff were under the cosh, I decided to make the upcoming INSET day a 'duvet day', the colloquial term for working from home. This was gratefully received by most of the staff and seen as exactly what it was: an attempt to make their lives easier. Unfortunately, this was not interpreted in the same way by everyone. Some part-time staff complained that as the duvet day fell on their day off, they did not get the benefit of this bed-based initiative and wanted to know when they would get their face-to-face time with a duvet.

Sometimes you just can't do right for doing wrong, and once, when we tried to praise staff by introducing a staff 'hero/heroine of the week' award, it rather unexpectedly unleashed hell. There were accusations of canvassing and favouritism, there were tears and tantrums from people who did not receive an award, as well as, unbelievably, from people who did. It really didn't help that I happened to receive one of the first awards (it cost me an arm and a leg to wangle that). We discontinued the practice after just half a term, but the scars remain.

MARCH 2014:
CREATING A CULTURE

When I first arrived at the school, I had been surprised to find that although the students were arranged into houses, other than sports day and an annual sponsored walk there was very little in the way of school tradition, so I started a drive to expand our house culture.

I began modestly, by offering a selection of enamel badges, stationery and drinks bottles in house colours. Things developed further with the introduction of a few new house competitions such as photography, poetry and dance, and this spurred on other staff to propose their own cups and competitions. It wasn't long before we had to buy cabinets to house all the new trophies, and we put them in a corridor that I subsequently named 'Quality Street'. Fired up by the positive response, I became consumed by a frenzy of house culture creation. I wrote lyrics to a school song and a leavers' poem and purchased house flags, mascots and an enormous silver house cup. I created an official initiation ceremony for new Year Sevens and Year Twelves, as well as a 'jacket handover' ceremony for the new Head Girls, based on the US Masters green jacket presentation. I embellished the existing school legends and myths and invented a few more.

In the meantime, Mr Gregory came up with the idea of a 'house shout', an inter-house singing competition. This is now one of the biggest and most exciting events in the house culture calendar and takes place on the afternoon of the last day of the summer term. Each house secretly rehearses a song to perform to the rest of the school and a panel of judges. It is taken deadly seriously, and both the students and staff have time out of lessons to practise their singing, their dance moves and to organize their costumes.

The event starts when the houses march behind their flags into the school hall and begin chanting and yelling their house mottos at each other. This has to be heard to be believed – the noise is incredible. I once used a sound meter from the physics department to measure the volume of noise produced and it was equivalent to that of a loud rock concert or a revving motorbike. Once through this period of potential auditory damage, the houses each strut their stuff to an enthusiastic audience. Watching the five sets of students and staff singing, dancing and giving it their all for the honour of their house is an incredibly uplifting experience.

One morning in March, I received a letter asking me to settle a dispute – between a duck and a giraffe – that had arisen out of this burgeoning house culture. I am not quite sure why, but the Wilkinson house mascot had always been a duck. For some reason, the newly appointed Head and Deputy Head of Wilkinson House decided they would change it to, of all things, a giraffe.

They conducted a superficial survey of opinion by whizzing around the Wilkinson form rooms one lunchtime before casually announcing this momentous change in their next house assembly. After a stunned silence, the assembly descended into chaos, and the next day I received a letter, written on behalf of all the Wilkinson Year Eights, complaining that the process had been undemocratic. The Head and Deputy Head of House responded by arranging another assembly during which they put forward the case for changing to a giraffe, and they put it to a vote. The giraffe camp won by about twenty votes, so I thought that would be the end of it, but the next morning I received a second letter from the Year Eights saying the process was still flawed because they had not been allowed to put forward the case for the duck. Cue another assembly, a passionate defence of the duck by the Year Eights, and another vote. Again the giraffe camp won, but this time by only two votes. The Head and Deputy Head of House realized that the duck sympathizers might now refuse to engage in giraffe-related activities, so they asked me to broker a compromise deal. The result for the students was a truce – an agreement to adopt both house mascots and a slightly confused identity going forward. The result for me was the pleasure of knowing how much they cared about their house.

The five houses are named after the previous headteachers, and however much I would love there to be a house called Smith (very much), the travesty is that I am the seventh Head. With our current five forms of entry, we are already tight for space, so there is definitely no room for me to bag a house of my own. This is very sad, and I find solace where I can.

I gain a little when I hear the students sing our school song, and Dr Coles told me of an occasion the previous weekend that warmed my heart. He had been out on Dartmoor with students training for the Ten Tors when a team had gone missing in the mire and the mist. There had been no contact with them for hours and, as the evening closed in and the weather worsened, he became very concerned for their safety. Just at the point he was considering calling the mountain rescue service and our emergency number (mine of course), he heard something in the distance. Faint at first, but gradually becoming stronger, he could hear the unmistakable sound of the school song rising up through the valley. Ten minutes later, singing at the top of their voices, the missing group emerged from the mist.

JUNE 2014:
A FORCE OF NATURE

Mrs Payne, our Head of PE, was a living legend both at school and in the local community. She had been teaching here for over thirty years and as well as being Head of PE she was Head of Year Nine. She was athletic, robust and kept herself ridiculously fit by running long distances, riding horses and working out in the school gym; she was even a veteran hockey international. Whatever the season, whatever the weather, she would only ever be found wearing shorts and had a 'can do, just get on with it' attitude, which she brought to bear on any student who dared try to evade PE.

Over the years she had seen every type of excuse letter imaginable. These included run-of-the-mill classics such as 'she's been up all night with an upset tummy', 'she has painful blisters where her new shoes have rubbed' or 'she has outgrown her PE kit', as well as more exotic ones like 'she is very weak from taking part in a charity fast'. Some of these sick notes also revealed a number of grandparents to be medical marvels, as they appeared to have passed away on more than one occasion.

Mrs Payne was having none of it. Despite their protestations she would make those waving sick notes join in with the rest to run cross-country in the rain, bounce alarmingly high on a trampoline and become intimately acquainted with a wide selection of contact sports. If a parent said their child had an upset tummy the night before, well that was the night before, wasn't it? If they had blisters on their feet, then she would give them a plaster, and if they had no kit, she would force them to wear smelly spares from lost property.

This attitude was to be commended, but it meant that I was constantly having to defend Mrs Payne's actions to disgruntled parents. Here is an example of the type of placatory response I would have to pen to the many furious emails I received:

Dear Mr and Mrs . . .

I am very sorry to hear about your daughter's leg. I hope that the soft tissues heal quickly and she can get back to normal as soon as possible. Have you tried some physiotherapy? I have gone over all aspects of your email with Mrs Payne and would like to convey her view of events with you.

There appeared to be some confusion, as Mrs Payne had wrongly believed that your daughter had thrown the discus previously, so had put her down to do it. When your daughter told Mrs Payne that this was not the case she entered her for the hurdles instead. Your daughter only had a few minutes to practise before the start of the race and this is when, unfortunately, she injured her knee by falling over one of the hurdles.

Mrs Payne said that she did examine your daughter's knee, but at that point there was no sign of swelling or bruising so she advised her to keep it moving and was of the opinion she would be fine to run in the race. Mrs Payne is adamant that she was shouting words of encouragement when your daughter began to lag behind the others and categorically denies swearing at your daughter. She does admit that when your daughter complained about her knee afterwards, she told her not to be a wimp, and for this she apologizes unreservedly. She says that on reflection she was a bit sharp and prickly, due to the pressure she had been put under at the tournament, but she certainly did not intend to ridicule or demean your daughter.

Mrs Payne would be the first to admit that her manner can be military-like and brusque, but it is usually with good humour, and she undoubtedly cares for the girls in her charge. I have made her acutely aware of the need for sensitivity in such situations and I hope that we can move on from this unfortunate incident. On a different point, nobody else has echoed your daughter's complaint about being violently jolted because Mrs Payne drove too fast across some speed humps, so I think it is possible that she had become over-sensitized as a result of her knee injury.

Thank you for contacting me about your concerns. Again, I wish your daughter a speedy recovery.

Best regards,
Dr Smith

There were many occasions that I had to act as an emollient between Mrs Payne and disgruntled parents and she did not make it easy for me. She was so passionate about getting all her students to take part in regular physical exercise that it often brought her into conflict with the parents of students who were less keen.

Aside from this, she was a Maverick, another of my big five teaching beasts. Most schools have a Maverick, a teacher who does not follow the rules – they are often, but not exclusively, PE or performing arts teachers and they do whatever it takes to get things done. If this involves taking short cuts, engaging in unusual practices or ignoring official procedures, then so be it.

They have very little regard for administration and consequently their lesson plans are minimal, their risk assessments are often lacking and their meeting minutes skeletal. Although they are not always bona-fide INSET Saboteurs, they have little time for strategic thinking or management gibberish, as it gets in the way of them getting things done. Consequently, they can often be seen whispering or texting during INSET sessions as they try to organize more important things. They do 'exactly what it says on the tin'; they get things done – it's just that they do it via unconventional means. This eccentric approach means they are often popular with students, who are thankful for a little bit of variety in their educational diet.

Very little got in the way of Mrs Payne getting things done. She would run the school's annual ten-mile sponsored walk in a fraction of the time it took everyone else to walk it, just so she could spend the rest of the day sorting out the PE store cupboard. To ensure she achieved an all-over body tan, she would surprise her Year Eleven students by sunbathing topless on the annual Spanish trip, and she never, ever, adjusted her speed when driving over speed humps in her rush to get from A to B.

This maverick approach generated extra work for me, as I was forever chasing up her paperwork, dealing with parent complaints or smoothing over staffing issues, so it might appear that the best course of action would have been to take her to task, clip her wings a little and get her to follow the rules. Not so. By now I had developed a much more holistic approach to people management. Before I reprimanded people, I now asked myself, 'On balance, is this person's contribution to our school positive or negative?' In the case of Mrs Payne, it was overwhelmingly positive.

Mrs Payne was a force of nature; she organized all the staff social activities, she kept the staffroom cupboards and fridge fully stocked and she compèred the PTA quiz. She remembered everyone's birthdays and made sure they received a small gift and card; she still remembers mine even though she left several years ago. She was always one of the first to volunteer to cover other people's bus duties or lessons and always one of the last to leave after helping clear up at the end of evening events.

She probably had the loudest voice west of Bristol, and although she was infamous for using it on slothful students who did not live up to her expectations, she had a good heart and cared about them all. She knew the name of every girl in the school and voluntarily organized shopping trips for them at Christmas, as well as arranging an annual ski trip and running a Year Elevens' water sports trip. There was very little she would not do for them.

When the scales are weighted so heavily in favour of a staff member like Mrs Payne, then I recommend you leave all the other minor niggles to the breeze.

JULY 2014:
THE SEVEN-YEAR ITCH

My first seven years in the post had passed by in the blink of an eye. Seven years as headteacher at a secondary school is a significant milestone because it means that the unfortunate Year Sevens who joined when you started the job have experienced all of their seven years of secondary education under your leadership. As this landmark approached, I took some time to pause and reflect on what I had or had not achieved during this time.

* Had I made sufficient progress or was there unfinished business here?
* Was I a hero yet?
* Was it time to move on to a second headship?

Well, we had certainly made progress in two high-profile areas: our academic results had improved considerably and, in 2011, Ofsted had upgraded us to 'outstanding'. In recognition of this achievement, I received a personalized letter from no less a luminary than Sir Michael Wilshaw himself. He congratulated me on achieving such a very high standard of practice and thanked me for all I was doing to raise standards and improve lives. I say personalized because I would like to think that after reading through our Ofsted report one evening, he had been moved to whip out his pen and write to me directly. I ignored all the signs clearly indicating it was the same letter received by the heads of all outstanding providers.

So, superficially things seemed to be going well, but the effects of austerity combined with the government's obsessive preoccupation with results was hindering the development of other, arguably more important areas of operation. We wanted to develop a much more balanced and holistic curriculum in order to protect our students' wellbeing. We were keen to get more girls into STEM subjects (science, technology, engineering and mathematics), to develop their leadership skills and make them more environmentally aware. I wanted my staff to develop themselves through high-quality training and to give them the time to reflect so they could deliver inspirational lessons. I wanted to facilitate staff so they could deliver a subject experience that went way beyond the standard curriculum with trips, visits, speakers, conferences, clubs, competitions and high-quality, meaningful work experience.

However, over the past seven years I had come to the slow realisation that achieving these things was not as straightforward as it had seemed when I had been climbing the management ladder. There were roadblocks, distractions and hurdles at every turn. Not enough money, not enough time, DfE interference, a mountain of administration, parental complaints, staffing issues and a daily inbox of nonsense that kept me firmly in Covey's 'not urgent, not important' box. My inability to do many of the things I felt were important meant that seeds of resentment with the system began to take root in my mind.

Progress aside, had I become the Hero Head I wanted to be? I considered some of the evidence:

* Over the past seven years, while some popular expletives had regularly featured in the same sentence as my name, the words hero, heavyweight, dynamic, charismatic and inspirational had not.
* Younger members of staff would sometimes refer to me as 'mate' or 'buddy'.
* I was challenged on three separate occasions by members of our casual staff wanting to know who I was and what I was doing on the school site. Although I was heartened by this excellent safeguarding practice, I was disappointed to find that they genuinely did not seem to know who I was.

On reflection, I could only conclude that there was still a

significant amount more work to do both in terms of school progress and in terms of Project Hero Head, so it wasn't going to be another headship for me. Rather, I would focus more on becoming an 'architect', and tortoise-like I would continue to play the long game. I therefore strapped myself in and got ready for a second seven-year stint.

Coincidentally, about the same time, the girls had a talk from a police recruitment officer who, over coffee afterwards, suggested I consider becoming a direct entry police superintendent. They were looking for leaders with experience to enter the profession at an elevated level. Now, I was pretty sure I would make a poor police superintendent, but I was tempted purely on the grounds that it would mean I would bag a public service royal flush of: healthcare, education and law enforcement. That must be a rare hand indeed. However, choosing to work in one public service is forgivable; to work in two is highly questionable; but to work in three? Well, that would mean you would have to be absolutely bonkers, wouldn't it?

I went as far as filling out the application form, but never quite got around to sending it.

Part Five: Headship II: The Belligerent Years

APRIL 2015:
THE RISE AND FALL

On the wall in my office hung a picture of Napoleon crossing the Alps painted by Jacques-Louis David in 1801. Napoleon is on horseback and is gesturing onwards, and the picture leaves no doubt as to his will to arrive at his goal and the inevitability of victory. As this term seemed to have gone so much better than the last, I secretly dared to liken myself to the Napoleon in this picture, spurring my troops on to greater things – brilliant, indestructible, flawless. The green shoots of heroism perhaps?

Luckily, in education you are never far from a situation that will help bring you rudely back down to earth. For me this came in the form of a calamitous assembly where I was given a timely reminder not to be such a conceited arse.

I genuinely enjoy giving assemblies. What's not to like? You get the chance to be the centre of attention, to tell some humorous anecdotes and, unlike in my usual social interactions where people tend to move off when I start talking, the audience is trapped.

In this assembly, I was trying to raise everyone's spirits and give them a boost at the end of a busy term. I was reflecting on the many things that had gone well during the preceding weeks, and what I had meant to say was, 'We have all had a ridiculous amount of success recently.'

Unfortunately, that is not what I said, and believe me when I tell you I have gone over the possible reasons why it didn't come out right many, many times. On reflection, it doesn't bear thinking about, so let's just say, for reasons unknown, what I actually said was: 'We have all had a ridiculous amount of sex recently,' quickly followed by 'success, success – a ridiculous amount of success.'

There were about 960 girls and 40 staff in the audience, and there was a short pause while they processed my words, after which the hall erupted with unbridled mirth. The merriment was fulsome and sustained, and they shrieked, hooted and chortled at will. It was all I could do to fix a neutral expression on my face and stare at my speech for the four minutes and forty-two seconds it took for exhaustion to kick in and for the merriment to abate. When they finally finished, I very slowly and very deliberately said, 'What I meant to say was we have all had a ridiculous amount of suc-cess recently,' heavily emphasizing the word suc-cess, but this just set off a secondary bout of giggling.

If there is a plus, then it is that a generation of students will remember one of my assemblies; on the minus side, not a week goes by without someone recounting my gaffe.

A short time afterwards, I replaced my picture of Napoleon with a different one painted by Paul Delaroche. It is of a small apartment room at the Palace of Fontainebleau on 31 March 1814. Napoleon sits slumped in a chair alone and out of shape. Disappointment and anger can be read on his face. His downfall is looming, the destruction of his empire has been decided and the monarchy will soon be restored. I find this picture really helps to keep me grounded.

Later in that year I recounted this story about my assembly to some visiting old girls, and one of them remembered a similar incident from when she was at the school many years previously. One winter it had snowed overnight, so the girl and her friends spent their lunchtime constructing snowmen. Unfortunately, they did this on part of the boys' school field because it had the deepest snow. The headmistress had seen this out of her window and called them into her office to lambast them for trespassing on the boys' land. As she ranted, they stood in silence looking suitably contrite right up until the moment she dismissed them with the line, 'Now get up to the boys' school and remove those undesirable erections immediately.'

SEPTEMBER 2015:

CRACK-A-JOKE

Many schools have a briefing for staff before morning registration. On the surface this appears to serve a mainly administrative function: notices for the day; reminders of deadlines; a chance to check pigeonholes and the cover list; that sort of thing. This would be a gross misrepresentation of the pivotal role that these ten to fifteen minutes play in the life of a school. For staff it's a time to catch up with each other; to let a tutor know their tutee is playing up; to have a quick chat with the teacher of a shared class; to alert the safeguarding lead of a concern; to share a moan about bus duty; and a thousand and one other crucial interactions before everyone gets sucked into the vortex of the school day.

As a headteacher, briefing is a daily opportunity to cement your ethos and vision. I recently became attracted to the idea of everyone standing to attention when I entered the room and repeating in unison our vision statement with one hand clasped to their chest. Fortuitously for staff, I have to pass my new picture of Napoleon on my way to briefing, so I'm brought back down to earth and settle for conveying my vision through my words and deeds instead.

I have worked in schools where this opportunity for positive reinforcement has been spurned. In one school, the staff were treated to a daily dressing-down. We traipsed all the way up to the staffroom only to be harangued about the many things we had not done, had not done properly or that we needed to do urgently. We sat in silence, cowed and subdued for ten minutes, before, like naughty children, we traipsed back out again.

In another school, the head was obsessed about staff being late for registration and she berated us all for this on a regular basis. If we are going to be role models, then yes, we should try to be on time for our tutees, but often the reason staff are late is because they are having the very interactions with other staff I mentioned before. This head, however, was having none of it, and would actually end vital conversations by walking up to people and slowly tapping her watch. As there were only ever a few people who were regularly late to registration for no good reason, this really was a poor strategy. I have found that you can improve punctuality dramatically if, when someone arrives late to registration, they find you sitting in their chair taking the register.

With this experience in mind, I decided this year I would try to make briefing as positive an experience as possible, so that at best the staff left inspired and uplifted, and at worst they at least had the chance to raise their blood-caffeine levels significantly. I introduced a new feature – the opportunity for us to all share a joke at the end of Friday's briefing. In a homage to the catchphrase from the well-known children's TV programme *Crackerjack*, I would announce, 'It's Friday, it's a quarter to nine and it's crack-a-joke time.'

This was the opportunity for any member of staff to tell a joke, the incentive being that if no one else did, then I would. As they really didn't like my jokes, it meant there was usually at least one volunteer. Once a joke had been told I would round it off by bashing a cymbal I'd rigged up with a drumstick. It was a win-win situation – if the joke was bad then everyone groaned; if the joke was good then they would all laugh. Either way they would all leave smiling, and in my mind, this must be one of the main aims of a briefing.

Conversely, you may suddenly need to call staff to attend an extraordinary briefing, and this is never a good thing because it usually means that storm clouds of some sort are gathering. Staff will assemble at such an event and whisper to each other in groups, nervously speculating on the possible reason for the meeting. Unusually, they instantly hush when you begin to speak. I have had to call extraordinary meetings twice for impending Ofsted inspections, twice for deaths in the school community, once for the imminent release of some adverse publicity and multiple times during the coronavirus pandemic.

By far the strangest of these meetings occurred early on during the pandemic, when I announced to staff that those who were deemed clinically vulnerable would now be entitled to work from home. In an instant a queue formed at my lectern, and despite me repeatedly telling everyone that I trusted their integrity, there seemed a real need from staff to get me to personally authenticate their clinical vulnerability. Perhaps it was because of my medical background, but whatever it was, one by one, they began to publicly disclose to me their medical details. This could be clearly heard not only by the rest of the queue, but also by the many staff yet to leave the briefing, most of whom were desperately pretending they were not listening when they absolutely were. We were treated to some fascinating details about kidney problems, asthma medication and the difficulties of controlling diabetes. We heard about weight issues, flu vaccine eligibility, two recent abdominal operations and a whole host of other ailments, maladies and illnesses. It reminded me of being in a hospital clinic, except that this clinic had a large live audience.

As I validated each of them in turn, it felt like I was giving them my blessing before a long journey. At one point, I think I did say, 'Go in peace' to an individual who had outlined a catalogue of medical issues. Little did any of us know that they were in fact about to go off on a long journey because it was many months before we saw them again.

OCTOBER 2015:
POLES APART

One weekend in the autumn term, a GP friend of mine asked me what I did all day long. She seemed unable to envisage any substantial or demanding activities that could fill up my diary. I eagerly jumped at the chance to trumpet the difficulties of headship, by giving her a quick run-down of a typical day, but she remained unimpressed. Keen not to let her go away believing my job was easier than hers, I spent the afternoon describing to her some of the challenges involved in keeping all of our stakeholders happy.

Although most of our stakeholders – the parents, the governors, the staff and the students – are broadly supportive of the things that we do, as each group is made up of a diverse range of individuals with differing opinions, it is inevitable that they will not always see eye to eye.

Extremes of opinion are par for the course on divisive issues such as vaccinations, mobile phone usage, contraceptive provision, nose piercings and industrial action by teachers, but stakeholders can also hold views that are poles apart in virtually every area of school operation.

One example is seen in the extent to which different parents feel the need to engage with the school. Despite our best efforts, there are some parents you just can't get into school and there are some you just can't keep out. The handful of parents who hand over responsibility for their daughter's education the minute they drop them off on the first day are always a worry. We may not see some of these again for the whole seven years that their daughter attends our school. Unfortunately, they can be the parents of the students who would most benefit from some sort of parental involvement in their schoolwork, behaviour or wellbeing. The pastoral teams are relentless in their efforts to engage these parents and even if they ultimately have no success in getting them across the threshold, they will at least check regularly that all is well at home.

On the other hand, there are a number of parents who have an almost pathological desire to be involved in the minutiae of school life. These parents can often be identified well before their daughter joins us because they will contact us with questions of an overly detailed nature.

* Q. Will my daughter be marked down for using a 2B pencil rather than the HB you have recommended?
* A. *Yes, this will deny her access to more than 30 per cent of the available marks.*
* Q. Her house colour is blue but the pencil case we have brought her is more teal than blue, is that acceptable?
* A. *Totally unacceptable. If she brings it in, she will be put into after-school detention for a year.*
* Q. Can you clarify section 5.2 subsection F of your Head Lice Policy?
* A. *No.*
* Q. What is the percentage of saturated fat in your organic flapjacks?
* A. *Pretty close to 100 per cent.*

* Q. Do you have any plans to start a Year Seven
  powerlifting club?
* A. *No need, and once you have felt the weight of
  your daughter's school bag you will know why.*

Some of these parents are, dare I say it, overprotective of their children. While I understand it's a natural desire to protect your offspring, parents that overzealously shield them from the routine bumps and scrapes of childhood actually hinder their chances of becoming the autonomous adults they want them to be. These are the classic 'helicopter' parents, and they endlessly contact us to manage every aspect of their daughters' lives. Can you keep her inside after school, as rain is forecast, and we don't want her getting wet at the bus stop? Can you get the canteen to reduce the amount of mayonnaise in their sandwiches as it is making her retch? Can you get the classmates who are having a party at the weekend to invite her as she is feeling left out? Can you make sure the classroom temperature doesn't dip below fourteen degrees because her legs get cold? Can you ban games of tag at breaktime as they are too rough? Can you make sure she receives a school prize because all her friends are getting one?

In addition to this, they are often found lurking in our foyer under the total misapprehension that I will personally be attending to their daughter's needs. For example, I once popped out of a crucial governors' meeting to collect some paperwork, only to be accosted in the foyer by one such parent. He told me his daughter had left one of her trainers behind after PE and, thrusting the other trainer into my hand, insisted that I immediately root through the changing rooms to retrieve it for her. Helicopter parents such as these create an onerous downdraught and require a considerable amount of staff time and effort to placate.

Differences of opinion between students can sometimes be difficult to resolve; after all, they are still learning how to rub along peacefully with each other. Differences of opinion between staff members can be even more difficult to resolve, particularly if they don't actually want to rub along peacefully with each other.

One Monday morning in the autumn term, it was discovered that two large boxes of chicken kievs had mysteriously disappeared from the kitchen. Now, unless there is an unexpected deathbed confession, we will probably never know the fate of those thirty-two chicken fillets pounded and rolled around cold garlic butter, then coated with eggs and breadcrumbs to be either fried or baked. Suffice to say there was a considerable difference of opinion among the catering staff over who had taken them, with accusations flying left, right and centre.

The ensuing investigation involved an investigating officer, witness statements, a timeline, a stocktake, interviews with the chief protagonists and their union reps, a tour of the walk-in freezer and the scanning of CCTV footage. The investigation report compelled me to set up a governors' hearing, which took a full morning to hear all the parties involved and examine the case. After all of this, there was no evidence to charge anyone for taking the kievs. Once again, more of my time had been wasted, the kievs were still missing and none of this effort had made an iota of difference to the education of our students.

School governance is also no stranger to differences of opinion and even the most cohesive of governing bodies will harbour opposing views. Never was this more starkly exposed than when our governors were asked to consider the suitability of a proposed text for the Year Eleven scripted drama performance.

Some governors regarded the award-winning play *Road* by Jim Cartwright to be an extremely effective and darkly funny portrayal of the desperation of people living in a deprived, working-class community under Thatcherism. Other governors regarded it as a controversial and offensive drama littered with obscenities and covering a variety of depressing and highly unsuitable themes.

The result was a long and painful censorship debate in which I attempted to broker some agreement between these diametrically opposed views. By explaining the script's context and emphasizing that we study controversial texts for sound educational reasons, which included exposing students to alternative life experiences, I eventually got them to agree that *Road* was acceptable. However, this result didn't come tariff free; they wanted me to add a brand-new policy to our ever-growing collection: an 'appropriate teaching material policy'.

One governor even enthusiastically suggested that we form some kind of live sub-committee, poised to spring into action whenever an expletive, defamation or lewd expression reared its ugly head. There were a few winces when, in an immediate deviation from the spirit of this newly suggested strategy, I told them I thought this idea was shite. Thankfully they didn't pursue this initiative any further; had they reviewed our current reading list, they would have been shocked to discover that the standard texts by luminaries such as Shakespeare, Chaucer and Steinbeck were chock-a-block with filth. It had also come to my attention that A-level drama students were using a text that included a reference to an unsavoury act with a sheep, and I really didn't have the time to investigate. Again, though, I had had to expend a lot of valuable time and effort trying to keep everyone happy.

Dealing with differences of opinion such as these is part of the daily treacle you must wade through as a headteacher before you get anywhere near to being heroic or, more importantly, improving teaching and learning. Sometimes it requires the deftness and diplomacy of an international negotiator and the patience of a saint to keep everyone happy.

Having spent some time outlining these types of challenge to my GP friend, I would like to think there was a well-deserved glint of admiration in her eye. It may well have been just a trick of the light.

MARCH 2016:

THERE IS MORE TO THIS THAN MEETS THE EYE

Because so much of the day-to-day job of a head involves problem solving, there is a real danger that you can come to view issues rather mechanically. You may see them as inconvenient glitches that need ironing out or complications that require clinical solutions. It is easy to begin to view the individual(s) concerned as the problem.

One such problem was a chemistry teacher called Mr Lacy. He was normally a very competent teacher and had unusually delivered a poor set of exam results. As I had oversight of the science faculty, I went in to observe one of his lessons. I was surprised to witness a lesson that lacked structure or interest. It was poorly delivered, and the students were confused, which led to some low-level disruption. Talking with the girls afterwards confirmed to me that the learning outcomes had not been met.

This was a situation that needed fixing, so I talked through with him what I saw as wrong and the practical actions he could take to improve. They were pretty basic – the sorts of actions you might be recommending to a trainee teacher rather than an experienced one. I painstakingly went through the points with him and arranged a follow-up lesson observation the next week.

At the end of my evaluation, he left looking somewhat

crumpled and beaten, but I brushed this aside because his lesson had been poor, and we couldn't have that, could we? I reasoned that once he had had a chance to reflect on my suggestions, he would pull himself together and the problem would be resolved.

Later in the week, I was rather irritated to see that he had requested the day off, for personal reasons, when I was due to observe him again. For goodness' sake, I thought – not only was he teaching badly but now he was avoiding my supportive solution. I sought him out to discover what was so important that he needed to miss his observed lesson. I was thinking along the lines of a dental appointment, MOT, boiler repair – the sort of thing that he could easily have arranged at another time – so I was completely taken aback by his reply.

'I am so sorry, but I need to go to the Egyptian Embassy,' he blurted out before bursting into tears.

He explained his tragic situation. His daughter had married an Egyptian man and they had a five-year-old daughter together. One day, while on holiday in Sharm-El-Sheikh, his daughter had returned to the hotel to find her brother-in-law but no sign of her husband and daughter. The brother-in-law informed her that her husband had taken their daughter off to be brought up in Cairo, and that she had been told her mother had abandoned her. This was the beginning of a living nightmare for Mr Lacy and his daughter, as they attempted find his granddaughter and bring her back to the UK. The issue was complicated by the fact that in Egypt there is no agreed international system in place to return children.

Mr Lacy had spent countless hours trying to help his daughter battle her husband, the Egyptian authorities, lawyers, red tape and the police in a desperate attempt to find his granddaughter. His daughter travelled to Cairo many times to try and find her, but in an immense, rambling metropolis of some twenty million people it was impossible. Day by day, this fruitless attrition had gradually worn Mr Lacy down until, just when he was at his wits' end, I had blundered in to observe his lesson. It wasn't that Mr Lacy couldn't teach; it was that there was something terribly awry in his personal life. I am ashamed to this day that I had failed from the very onset to explore the intensely human element of his problem. I belatedly offered him all the limited support we had at our disposal and never again deigned to tell him how to teach. Unfortunately, Mr Lacy never managed to locate his granddaughter, and as he recently passed away, tragically he never got to see her again.

I had learnt a painful lesson once again that there is often more to a situation than meets the eye, and you need to gather all the information before you embark on a knee-jerk response. I resolved that in the future I would try much harder to seek out the root cause of a problem before I rushed in to treat the symptoms.

JUNE 2016:
WHEN I WAS YOUR AGE

A recurring belief of older generations is that growing up nowadays is far easier than in the past. After a particularly fractious half-term holiday, when both my children displayed a complete lack of appreciation for their fantastic, sparkling lives, I became a paid-up member of this school of thought. My level of irritation was such that, despite an extended rant to Caroline, I remained extremely disgruntled. Unable to contain the emotional wave this generated, I sought release by lambasting 600 of the younger generation in an assembly on my return to school. The assembly was entitled: 'When I was your age, things were very different'.

In it, I outlined the many ways in which my childhood had been tougher than theirs. I pointed out that, unlike them, I hadn't received constant technological stimulation, so I'd learnt to amuse myself for hours on end with something as simple as a stick, a piece of string, or a particular favourite, the humble paperclip. There had been no fancy food when I was growing up; I had been fed beef dripping instead of kale and quinoa, and I had no idea what an avocado was.

As I warmed to my theme, I clasped my hands behind my back and paced back and forth across the stage. The 'Blakey's' on my brogues (shout-out to Mr Freely) made a rather agreeable clicking noise, and when I reached the edge of the stage, I spun briskly around on one foot, before striding back in the opposite direction. I was so engrossed in this walking monologue that I was oblivious to the audience. I continued in this vein for some time until, halfway through one circuit, it dawned on me that something truly terrible had happened. It was with utter horror that I realized I had morphed into my father!

I had just delivered the very same lecture he had given me a thousand times. Worse than that, my hands were clasped in an identical pose, and I had even replicated his trademark one-footed spin. It was a Greek tragedy all of my own making, and something I have still not fully recovered from. I know it happens to all of us as part of the cycle of life, but it is still quite a shock to discover you have officially become an irritating old fart. There was no coming back from such a performance, although I did briefly consider growing an in-vogue hipster beard to help regain some of my credibility. That was until Caroline correctly pointed out that I was likely to end up resembling one of the characters from *The Hobbit*, so in the end, my attempt at redefining my image was limited to my next assembly, the title adapted slightly from the original quote by James Dean: 'I dream as if I'll live forever. I live as if I'll die today.' Unfortunately, the damage had been done.

Although I think that growing up in the past was physically more demanding than it is today, it is also clear to me that the younger generation are under far greater mental strain than we ever were. They feel increasingly pressured from a world full of rampant consumerism and celebrity culture. It's a world in which they must strive for physical perfection and stunning success on all fronts. When they fail to meet these expectations, many are not equipped to cope, and can become ill.

According to the Department for Education, in 2017, more than one in three teenage girls suffered from anxiety or depression – a rise of 10 per cent in a decade. Our students are the first generation to have lived their lives fully in a digital age. They have no escape from the addictive, twenty-four-hour online culture constantly reminding them of the unobtainable expectations of society, or from the relentless stream of peer judgement via social media. Many lack the direction and stability that faith and family previously provided, and if that was not enough, even the climate is changing. Physically, things are no better either; the stark increase in childhood obesity and associated diabetes has been described as a modern-day epidemic.

The problem for our students is that previous generations have created a world where staying healthy is surprisingly difficult and increasingly unusual. When I was growing up, we ate lots of vegetables, walked or cycled everywhere and the internet had not been invented. Our teenagers' lives are very different, and they face daily challenges to their physical and mental wellbeing.

Our initial attempts to counter this trend resulted in an explosion in the number and range of support personnel we employed. We utilized a whole host of pastoral heads, counsellors, nurses, safeguarding officers, SEND personnel, mental health practitioners, student mentors, catch-up coordinators and pupil premium champions, along with help from a wide range of external agencies. Remarkably, it did not matter how much we increased our capacity, it was never enough. The demand always seemed to grow to swamp our supply. I realized that this was because our army of pastoral operatives were only really treating the symptoms of the issue and not its causes, and that we needed to head upstream in an effort to staunch this flow of ill health.

It seemed to me that the principal challenge for schools was to rebalance academic learning with emotional wellbeing. To do this, I decided to implement a whole school health curriculum based on the work of geographer Dan Buettner at *National Geographic*. He had studied the five places in the world where people live the longest and have low levels of chronic disease. These places are found in Japan, Italy, Greece, Costa Rica and California, and are known as Blue Zones.

The researchers were surprised to discover that, although these long-lived communities were many miles apart, they had similar habits in common. For example, they all had a strong sense of purpose and belonging. Family was the priority around which they built their lives. They set aside time in the day when they could escape the commotion of life, and they had routines that helped shed stress. They ate moderate amounts of fresh, unprocessed local produce, consisting mainly of plants. They did not go to the gym or run marathons; their exercise came from the movement involved in their daily lives. They would walk to most places, and they used the stairs. They did household chores by hand, and they dug, hoed, weeded and harvested their gardens.

As moving our students to a Blue Zone was impossible, we instead developed a modified version of the Blue Zone habits – our school's own 'Ten Healthy Habits'. I hoped that it might make them not only healthier, but happier as well.

To realize this ambition, we focused our curriculum as much as possible on health. We created a quarter-mile circuit through our grounds, and students were expected to walk around it a certain number of times each half-term. We asked students to choose four friends to form social support groups based on the lifelong friendship groups in Japan known as Moai. We provided t'ai chi and yoga sessions. We introduced a no cake/biscuits policy in lessons and we had Blue Zone food choices in the canteen. We also introduced dozens of other activities, including a gardening club, organized lunchtime student games and mid-lesson movement sessions, as well as having a quiet/meditation area and creating a Blue Zone recipe book. Through these types of curricular experience, we aimed to encourage our students to make small persistent changes that would gently nudge them towards lifelong healthy habits.

Our programme gathered some interest – we were asked to present at conferences, it was featured in an article in the *Times Educational Supplement* and we were given the opportunity to outline the programme to the schools minister. However, the wholescale adoption of this sort of curriculum is problematic, as it requires:

* The freedom to escape the straitjacket of an exam-orientated curriculum.
* The funding to staff a major cross-curricular programme of physical and mental wellbeing.

If this was implemented, I believe that not only could schools help counter the rising tide of childhood illness, but it would be the single most important investment any government could make.

JULY 2016:
ISN'T IT TIME YOU LEFT?

In July 2016, Ms Neal, our longest-serving member of staff, finally took the plunge and retired. Having joined the school in 1978, she had been here for thirty-eight years. When she started, the Bee Gees were focused on staying alive and Rod Stewart wondered whether you thought he was sexy. Personally, I didn't, but as I was fourteen at the time, I was mainly concerned with the fact that my voice had not broken. By the time Ms Neal left, Justin Bieber was telling her to love herself. During her time at the school, Ms Neal had been a history teacher, Head of Careers and Deputy Head of Sixth Form. I have retrospectively created a more accurate job description than the one she would have received back in 1978, when she was deciding whether to apply for the post.

Dear Ms Neal,

Thank you for your interest in the position here at our school. I have outlined the main elements of the role below as well as our expectations of you were your application to be successful.

Once appointed you will be expected to:

* Drag yourself through the school gates on 7,223 separate occasions.
* Deliver over 30,000 of your own lessons and cover another 1,440 for absent colleagues.
* Sit through 3,610 assemblies (including a rather embarrassing one where the head talks about how much sex everyone is having).
* Write 3,500 very positive UCAS references irrespective of the calibre of the student.

* Receive 768 letters/cards of thanks and praise if you turn out to be popular, but just a handful if you are not.

* Suffer 256 staff meetings, 42 that involve heckling and 3 that feature a slow handclap.

* Endure 190 INSET days including 5 INSET weekends described by management as 'really good' and by everyone else as 'a living nightmare'.

* Attend 152 parents' evenings involving 5,968 reasonable parents and 48 very unreasonable ones.

* Catch 56 colds and 4 cases of diarrhoea and vomiting, courtesy of your students.

* Take part in fire practice 96 times, 29 of them in the rain.

* Be told on 16 separate occasions that the homework you have set has been eaten by a dog.

* Escort 46 drunken students out of the toilets at the Leavers' Ball.

* See off 7 Ofsted inspections, all of which use different assessment criteria.

* Despair over 16 subject specification changes.

* Find yourself alone on bus duty 16 times after flimsy excuses/lies from your colleagues.

* Be locked in your room by the caretaker while working late, once by mistake and once deliberately.

* Suffer 3 headteachers, the last of whom wants to be a hero.

*   Receive a modest gift token and an orchid in a
    pot after 38 years of dedicated service.

If, having carefully read the details above, you still
wish to apply please send your CV and written letter
of application to the headteacher at the address above.

With the benefit of hindsight, I wonder whether she would
have applied. Either way, these many experiences provided
Ms Neal with an insight into education that came in rather
handy for the other role she held – a role that for some
reason no one had thought to tell me about. I knew she was
the school representative for the Association of Teachers
and Lecturers (ATL), which was the teaching union most of
our staff belonged to. What I didn't know was the full extent
of her involvement with the union.

Shortly after I joined the school, we were chatting in
the corridor when she casually slipped a bombshell into
the conversation by mentioning that she had recently been
elected as the National President of the union. Despite being
taken aback by the magnitude of this revelation, I heartily
congratulated her, but I walked away feeling uneasy about
what this might mean for my grand plans. Did this mean
I was likely to meet union resistance to the changes I'd
planned in contentious areas like performance management
or lesson observation? Would my plans be blocked by
staff that now had unfettered access to the president of a

120,000-strong teaching union? It felt like my wings were going to be clipped before I had even got started.

Thankfully, my fears were groundless. In fact, Ms Neal became a vital component in my planning process. For anything that might be deemed controversial, I would go to her in the first instance, and she would gently point out the elements of proposals that might cut across union guidance. She would signpost me to relevant good practice, ensure I consulted appropriately and prevented me from making any major political mistakes. I am convinced I was able to make many more positive changes working with her than if I'd been left to blunder around on my own. She was uncommonly reasonable, and we worked in harmony together right up until the day she finally retired.

DECEMBER 2016:
ARE YOU STILL EAR!

The culture of presenteeism is rife in teaching, and I have been a slave to it for most of my career. I have always needed to be the first in every morning (about 6:50 a.m. if you're asking) and for twenty years and 223 days, like a chump, I never took a day off sick. I don't know how I got sucked into this way of thinking. I think it was partly the sense of guilt I got if I was not working and partly my desire to be an indestructible Hero Head.

I realized rather late in my career that this is a very poor strategy. Headship is a demanding job, both physically and mentally, and as you get older it becomes even more tiring. Maintaining the long hours and a full attendance record had become like a millstone around my neck. It meant I would not take time off for rest or recovery because I didn't want to lose my shiny presenteeism crown. There must have been occasions where my judgement was clouded by infectious agents and it is highly likely that, as well as subjecting my colleagues to my impaired judgement, I generously shared my microbes with them, too.

Luckily, I was released from this situation at the end of the Christmas term, when I got an infection in my ear causing it to swell up like a balloon. It went an angry dark red and looked like a rubber joke ear – much to the amusement of everyone who saw it. My doctor insisted I stopped working, prescribed me high-dose antibiotics and told me that if the swelling spread, I should go straight to the hospital. To help me assess any further spread, she drew a line around the margins of the redness with permanent marker pen, which provided further amusement for everyone.

While I was off recovering, I had the time to properly reflect on my presenteeism strategy and realized very late in the day that it is not about being there all the time – there are no prizes for hours at school, for being first in or last to leave – it is all about outcomes. There is no direct correlation between hours invested and positive outcomes. Taking time off to rest and recuperate is likely to make you more efficient in the long run. Since this revelation I have become a little more relaxed about the need to be omnipresent, and it feels like a weight has lifted from my shoulders.

To be clear though, I don't want this to be misinterpreted. I have no truck with the small number of individuals who have a ridiculously low threshold for taking time off. Over the course of my career, members of staff have managed to look me directly in the eye while telling me they had been unable to come into work because they had indigestion, their pond was covered in algae, they dropped a can of beans on their big toe or their pet lizard was unwell. These are the same people who never volunteer to cover someone else's bus duty, who will happily leave you putting chairs away at the end of a long parents' evening or feel they have no role to play in getting a thousand students into the assembly hall. They often suffer from it's-above-my-pay-grade-itis, I-finish-at-three-forty-five-osis or it's-not-on-my-job-description-emia – sometimes all of them.

FEBRUARY 2017:
LAUREN GREENWAY

Lauren Greenway was a delightful Year Eight girl. I remember when she first arrived at our school as keen as mustard in Year Seven. She was wide-eyed and willing, eager to embrace the new experiences our school had to offer and determined to squeeze the juice out of every single day. I'm not sure whether it has been scientifically studied, but students like Lauren have a kind of palpable 'glow' about them; they radiate an infectious vitality that is so utterly uplifting that it makes teaching them an absolute pleasure. As well as this, Lauren was kind, caring and fiercely loved by her friends.

Out of the blue, one Thursday in late February, Lauren collapsed at home and was rushed to hospital. On investigation it was discovered she had suffered a brain haemorrhage as the result of undiagnosed acute leukaemia. She was swiftly transferred to the regional paediatric trauma centre in Bristol, so that surgeons could operate. Despite their best efforts they were unable to save her, and tragically, on Saturday morning, she passed away. On the following Monday I had to deliver the one assembly that no headteacher ever wants to give, and I discovered how bloody clumsy and inadequate words can be to express something as profoundly unfair as the death of a student.

At twelve years old, Lauren was too young to die, and her death must have caused her parents and sister Ellie, one of our Year Tens, the most unimaginable pain. She was also an integral part of our school family, and her death rocked our community to its core. At that age our students believe they are invincible and that their sparkling lives, so full of possibility, will go on forever; having this belief so cruelly challenged left them feeling shocked, numb and angry.

All I could really do was to let them know that the feelings they had were okay and that it was important to acknowledge how they felt by talking to their friends, teachers and parents. Most things pale into insignificance when compared to something like this, so I encouraged them to put aside any petty insecurities, squabbles and dissatisfactions in order to support each other and to reach out to those most affected. I am proud to say that they did this in spades, and there was an outpouring of love for the family and friends of Lauren as the school community came together in its shared grief.

I later represented the school at Lauren's packed funeral service, along with other members of staff and some of her closest friends. Her family showed an almost impossible dignity throughout, and the service was a real celebration of their wonderful daughter. In tribute to Lauren's vibrant nature, and in defiance of the sadness of the occasion, they had even chosen her a bright pink coffin – her favourite colour.

In the weeks going forward, Lauren's family, form and friends discussed how they would best like to remember her. Her form created a memory board displaying pictures of all the fun times they'd had together, and they zealously transferred it to each of their new form rooms as they passed up through the school. We also planted a cherry tree in her honour in the inner triangle just outside my office. I pass it every day and I am heartened to see that it continues to grow vigorously and delivers a riot of pink blossom every spring.

The best memorial to Lauren however was the creation of a new set of yearly awards. Time and time again, the key characteristic that came up when people were remembering Lauren was her kindness. We therefore decided to create a set of 'kindness cups' in her memory. These are given out on prize day to the girl in each form who is voted by her peers as most consistently showing the qualities of compassion, kind-heartedness and consideration for others. Students (and their parents) are understandably proud if they receive any of our usual awards, but they seem particularly proud if they receive a kindness award.

It is difficult to see any good in such a sad event as Lauren's untimely death, but I do feel that our school community became a little more connected as a result, and that each of us became more appreciative of our own lives. Moreover, not only is Lauren now remembered every year, but kindness is formally celebrated throughout our school. As legacies go, hers is a good one.

JUNE 2017:

THE DISAPPEARANCE OF DR HALLIDAY

There are some staff who will not engage in any task not specifically stated in their job description. These staff are also unlikely to deviate from their specified start or finish times. They will never come in early to help deal with a crisis and, at the end of the day, they will either leave on the dot or earlier. This adherence to the letter of their contract is their absolute right, as they do not get paid for doing any more than this, but the problem is the needs of the students inevitably spill out beyond such artificial boundaries and require, within reason, a degree of flexibility and goodwill.

Thankfully, despite the occasional 'Slopey Shoulders' finding their way into education, the profession seems to attract the type of people who pay little heed to their job descriptions and do whatever it takes to get things done. As schools are dependent on this goodwill, it is imperative that leaders take great care not to abuse it. One person who was both hyper-flexible and full of good will on a daily basis was my personal assistant Mrs Rumbelow. Although her official title was 'Headteacher's PA and Admissions Officer', this does not provide any real insight into the nitty-gritty of her role, and I believe that if I had properly explained the full scope of the job to her at interview, she may well have turned us down.

Apart from the need to be a fierce gatekeeper and beat

back all the unwanted emails, letters and visitors I receive, she is also my purchaser-in-chief. Over the years she has been asked to source a wide variety of items including huge packs of paper doilies, crates of mulled wine, a starting pistol, a soft plastic replica hand, a Father Christmas outfit, several tons of manure and a bandstand. Despite there being no mention of catering in the job description, the catering demands placed upon her have included the need to cut 1,500 slices of cake during awards week and to provide a vegan meal for the visiting schools minister and his team.

She was physically challenged when asked to help strim and clear a large bank of brambles on the edge of our site, and technically challenged when asked to fix the minibus doors that had jammed. Transport isn't part of her brief either, but one year she secured a replacement bus service when our bus company went bust, and every winter she will watch the local traffic cameras when it snows. Specifically, she watches the Splatford split and the wobbly wheel traffic cameras (both well-known local road junctions) to see whether our school buses and staff are going to make it in from Exeter. By default, she is the first port of call for any younger students found sobbing in the foyer after missing their bus home.

During her time with us she has been abused by angry parents, harassed by locals and, once, very publicly bad-mouthed during an appeal hearing at the town hall. This was both unexpected and a bit unfortunate, as I had only invited her along for a bit of company. She had to coordinate our response to an unexploded World War Two bomb discovered near the hotel on our London trip, and one Christmas she had to dress up in an elf costume. Perhaps, however, the task furthest removed from her job description occurred during a visit from our local community police officer.

This over-enthusiastic young man jumped at the chance to give me an impromptu demonstration when I casually asked about the taser peeking out from his police vest. To properly demonstrate the use of its red-dot laser sight he needed a volunteer target, and it was as he was training the red-dot laser neatly onto Mrs Rumbelow's forehead that I realized this was probably a task too far. I have since pinned the taser sticker the officer gave us onto our noticeboard as a testament to Mrs Rumbelow's helpfulness.

In short, Mrs Rumbelow does whatever needs to be done and calmly copes with everything that is thrown at her. She does this because it is in her nature. Others will also go beyond the call of duty for you for a different reason, because at some point in the past you have forged a positive bond with them. This can be a shared experience, either good or bad, where together you were involved in something memorable, challenging, exciting or intense.

The previous summer, nine colleagues and I had completed the Three Peaks Challenge, which involved climbing the three highest peaks in England, Scotland and Wales within a twenty-four-hour period. It was no small task and involved vigorous training. Despite the physical and mental challenge, together we summited all three peaks against the perfect backdrop of blue skies and stunning views. It was a truly memorable adventure. Every so often, when we pass each other in the corridor, our steely eyes will briefly meet and we feel the unspoken bond that we forged high in the mountains. The result is that my ex-companions are much more willing, within reason, to help out if I need them to do something extra, just as I am willing to put myself out for each of them.

Another such example of sharing a positive past came about this term when a group of staff decided to complete the Perambulation of Dartmoor. This involves walking the fifty miles around the ancient boundary of Dartmoor. This time the weather was terrible; it was blowy with thick fog. Almost immediately we lost our way and stayed lost for a good three hours. I probably need to concede at this point that I was navigating, but in my defence, those streams look devilishly similar in the mist. We eventually got back on track and were gamely trudging through thick bracken when I noticed that Dr Halliday, who was bringing up the rear, had disappeared. Quickly striding back through the bracken, I stumbled upon her head and shoulders sticking up out of a deep hole in the peat. The team gathered round and we tried to pull her out, but she was stuck tight. Everyone was laughing and joking about the situation until a look of panic spread across her face. 'There is something moving underneath my feet,' she squeaked.

Between us we finally managed to heave her out, and in the process created a little bit of 'positive past' together. We peered back down the hole and, five feet below, there was a sheep looking back up at us. It had somehow fallen down there and got itself stuck. It took us a good half-hour to dig it out and drag it up by its horns.

Once your colleagues have rescued you from a peat bog, you are much more likely to help them out, so that a future conversation might go something like this:

> 'Dr Halliday . . .'
>
> 'Yes.'
>
> 'Do you remember when you disappeared on the Perambulation?'
>
> 'Yes.'
>
> 'And it was me that noticed you were missing and came back and found you?'
>
> 'Yes.'
>
> 'And if I hadn't then you might still be there, but probably without any toes because that sheep would have nibbled them off?'
>
> 'Yes.'
>
> 'Well, I was wondering whether you would do my bus duty . . .'

I would recommend creating as much of a shared positive past as possible. This is not confined to extreme challenges; being in a school quiz team, part of a cookery club, having a skittles night or an INSET weekend will usually suffice, although it's probably best to avoid a year group sleepover. The more experiences, the more bonds, and the more bonds the more goodwill, and the more goodwill the better the education you can provide.

Sometimes these bonding experiences are thrust upon you – an Ofsted inspection, a bereavement in the school community, funding pressures or a global pandemic. When the chips are down, the staff you have forged positive bonds with are the ones who will suddenly appear by your side.

FEBRUARY 2018:
THE PEOPLE'S CHAMPION

Back in 2007, I was introduced to a teacher who was part of the fabric of the school. Gill Baker was a geography teacher who had worked at the school for decades prior to my arrival. Although she had officially retired back in 2004, there had rarely been a week since when she had not been in school helping out in geography, covering lessons or teaching sex education.

Initially we were wary of each other. On my part I had been told that she hated authority and 'the system' and had been quite awkward in the past with the senior team. I quickly discovered she had little truck with rules, protocols or policies and very much did her own thing. Students loved her for this non-conformity and also because despite being a pensioner, she was outrageously forthright in her sex education sessions. On her part I think she was wary about the direction in which this new 'wet behind the ears' headteacher might take the school.

However, the more I got to know Gill, the more I realized that she was the very best of us. She did things on her own terms not because she was part of the awkward squad, but because she was what I call a People's Champion, the last of my big teaching beasts. The driving force of a People's Champion is to do just that, to champion people, whether it be the students, the staff or the disadvantaged and vulnerable sections of the community. Their determination to do this means they won't let red tape get in the way of the welfare of others, and they are often the unapologetic voice-piece of people who are less represented or less able to stand up for themselves.

At first sight, a People's Champion might appear to be automatically resistant to any management changes you may wish to implement but, more often than not, they are simply promoting the welfare of others. They are quick to point out the human cost of the plans you have hatched. For example, your splendid new reporting format may well better inform parents of their child's progress, but it would also mean that teachers would have to spend every spare minute of the summer term writing reports. Your new uniform regulations may well result in a smarter-looking, more homogeneous set of students, but its cost will be a stretch for families on lower incomes. Over time, instead of regarding these types of observations as a hindrance, I came to view them as another vital part of my planning process. Teachers like Gill reminded me that there were always people on the end of the strategic decisions I made, and taking this into account upfront increased my chances of success.

Gill championed some of the more marginalized sections of society; for instance, she had a connection with the local Bangladeshi community and helped their families out with the school application process, as well as providing them with tuition in English.

Another group she took under her wing was our fledgling LGBTQ+ community. She nurtured it from a low-key selection of self-conscious students to a vibrant, forty-strong, loud and proud group. The world of gender identity was rapidly changing, and Gill made it her business to keep me informed of the latest developments. She provided me with a list of the various gender identities. I studied this information with interest and, the next time we met, asked her to clarify a few of the definitions, as I was having trouble distinguishing between some of the groups. Once she had put me right on the differences between the genderfluid, pangender and nonbinary groups she went on to clarify some of my other misconceptions. By the end of our meeting not only did I feel considerably better informed but it had opened up an ongoing and regular dialogue between the both of us.

Gill continued to champion the LGBTQ+ group, and it was she who made sure I gave some thought to how we were going to support our transitioning students, how we should approach the use of pronouns in school and how we could deliver an LGBTQ+ inclusive curriculum. The last time I saw Gill was in February of 2021, when we talked through her latest plans for the group. The next week, before she had a chance to put any of these plans into place, we received the sad news that, at the age of seventy-four, she had passed away peacefully in her sleep. She had continued to champion people right to the last, and if ever there was an example to our students of a generative life well lived, then it was hers.

People's Champions are the advocates of the waifs and strays of the school community. These are the students (and occasionally staff) who struggle to fit in for whatever reason. They are the students you see walking around on their own at lunchtime or sitting by themselves in the form rooms. They are the last ones to be picked for teams in PE and the ones left out when classes are asked to get into groups. Thankfully, these students are routinely brought into the welcoming embrace of a People's Champion.

JUNE 2018:
THINK FOR YOURSELF, THEN
ACT ON IT!

Unsurprisingly, our hundred-year-old school motto is a Latin one. It is *Aude Sapere*, which roughly translates as 'dare to be wise'. I prefer to translate it as 'dare to think for yourself', although teaching students how to think for themselves is not always easy. They prefer certainty, familiarity and structure, so we need to get them to routinely think about things with a critical eye, to formulate their own ideas and consider a range of different, alternative actions. This requires us to create an environment in which students feel comfortable voicing their developing thoughts without fear of ridicule or failure, and this needs to happen as often as possible across all lessons and activities. They will not think for themselves after a one-off afternoon workshop, but rather through a persistent and pervasive culture of encouragement.

Once they have dared to think for themselves, they then need to act on it. All our students were agitated about climate change, and while some followed through by making changes to their lifestyle, writing letters to MPs and attending protests, others did little more than liking a few posts on social media. As well as talking the talk, we need to get them to walk the walk. One of our Year Twelve students who did just this, wrote the following opening paragraph in her university personal statement:

I was affronted by the refugee crisis and so volunteered at the Calais Refugee Camp, 'the Jungle', for a week. While at the camp, I was involved in making drinks and playing games with refugees. Having survived horrific journeys, it was therapeutic for refugees to talk about their experiences. On return to the UK, I supported those in need in my local community, through raising awareness of the local homeless shelter.

I think you will agree this is a step up from banner waving and mouse clicking. Another student who dared to think for herself and act upon it was one of our quieter girls, Ellie Pollock. Ellie was a massive fan of the band The Killers, and she had managed to get her hands on a ticket to see them play at the Liberty Stadium in Swansea. She had watched many clips of their previous of concerts and seen that on occasion they would invite a fan up on stage to play along with them. Ellie was determined that, in Swansea, she was going to be that person. She spent hours relentlessly practising a track called 'A Dustland Fairytale' on the keyboard and made an enormous sparkly banner to draw attention to herself at the gig. She arrived ridiculously early and queued for hours in the heat to guarantee she would be near the front.

During the concert she waved the banner frantically every time the lead singer Brandon Flowers looked in her direction, and then . . . the unbelievable happened. He invited her to join him on stage to accompany him as he sang 'A Dustland Fairytale'. Standing behind the keyboard, right at the front and centre of the stage, she played the song alongside Brandon to 20,000 cheering fans. If that wasn't enough, she sang the last part of the song in a duet with him. When she came back in on Monday, she didn't mention anything about this incredible experience to any of the staff. It was only when her mum emailed me a link to the clip that we became aware of how she really had 'thought for herself', and as a result had made her dream come true.

The students who are able to think for themselves and then act upon it are often the ones who become confident risk-takers. They tend to be more resilient, more creative and more self-assured, so it is definitely something we should be encouraging. Aside from climate change and the refugee crisis, the two other significant events that have recently galvanized our students into action are the tragic murders of George Floyd in America and Sarah Everard here in the UK.

It has been really heartening to see so many students reacting strongly to social issues such as these. Primarily because these topics deserve their attention, but also because having been a keen activist in my youth, it was encouraging to see a new generation of young people becoming passionate about social justice. The first full day Caroline and I spent in each other's company was on the London poll tax march of 1990. I like to tell people that when our eyes first met across a smoke-strewn Trafalgar Square, it was love at first sight, but the truth is somewhat less romantic. It was while we were cowering from the rioting in the doorways of Soho that it crossed my mind that the small but fierce protester sheltering next to me was really quite wonderful.

In the wake of the 2020 death of George Floyd, the African American man murdered by a white police officer during an arrest, our students showed their support for the Black Lives Matter movement in various ways. They led assemblies on discrimination, attended rallies and vigils, set up a pressure group and asked us to review our reading lists to better reflect a diverse society. They hoped that such actions would, in some small way, help improve racial understanding.

The 2021 murder of thirty-three-year-old Sarah Everard, as she walked home from a friend's house one evening in south London, also affected our girls greatly. Coming on the back of the Me Too movement, it further highlighted to them the misogyny and sexual harassment women frequently have to endure. Several of the more active students decided to make a log of the aggravation they were subjected to on a daily basis, and the results were appalling. They received harassment from the minute they stepped outside their front doors: walking to school, on public transport, at school, in their part-time jobs and out in town in the evening and at weekends. They encountered it everywhere, and even if they managed to avoid face-to-face hassle, they could receive it online.

The 2021 Ofsted review into sexual harassment in schools concurred with our girls' findings reporting that 'sexual harassment and online sexual abuse, such as being sent unsolicited explicit sexual material and being pressured to send nude pictures ('nudes'), are much more prevalent than adults realize. Nearly ninety per cent of girls said being sent explicit pictures or videos of things they did not want to see happens a lot, sometimes to them or their peers, with the figure rising to ninety-two per cent for sexist name-calling.'

So endemic are these harmful sexual behaviours that some young people now consider them to be normal. However, just how this makes many of our students feel was eloquently outlined to me in an email from one of my Year Nines:

> Every day we are subjected to sexist, racist, homophobic or derogatory slurs. Just coming into school on the bus, my friends and I have to endure these abusive comments, and they are not simply 'banter', they are explicit and offensive.
>
> Girls should be able to feel confident and secure about engaging in their lives without the fear of sexual abuse. Expecting us, as teenagers, to address these issues is unreasonable and unfair. We should be spending our time on our studies or extra-curricular activities, not taking the lead on

these fundamental issues of equality and respect. We simply want to feel safe and equal to our male peers, going to school and about our business. This is not an unreasonable position to hold. Currently, we regularly feel intimidated, belittled and disrespected. We need to feel confident that our educators and adults are taking this issue seriously and taking adequate steps to address it. We want the perpetrators to be held to account and those who do not partake in such behaviour to call out those that do. Until this happens no female will ever feel equal or safe within our society.

This heightened awareness of the scale of the problem has rightly pushed the issue to the top of the agenda of schools, forcing them to, among other things, review their Relationship, Sex and Health education programmes and secure high-quality training for teachers.

While schools will undoubtedly do what they can to tackle this culture, it cannot be done in isolation. Trying to unpick student social media trails is an impossibility for school staff – they have neither the expertise nor the time. Help is required at a national level through the development of an Online Safety Bill that will help protect children from harm on social media platforms.

There is also a need to address such behaviours in the workplace. This had become glaringly apparent to us previously, when a chef in the kitchen where one of our students worked was cajoled by his workmates to expose himself to her 'for a laugh'.

Not willing to allow such behaviours to become normalized, one of our students, with the help of Mrs Browne, our Head of Sixth Form, managed to secure a meeting with Victoria Atkins MP, the Minister for Safeguarding. She called on her to consider a workplace charter to help address the sexual harassment students face in places of work. It is so encouraging that some of our students are willing to think for themselves and then act on it.

FEBRUARY 2019:
THE FILTER IS CLOGGED

Another important role of a head is to filter out the bulk flow of nonsense directed at your staff. If they had to jump to the tune of all the latest educational research – Ofsted's pet topics, government directives or IT fads – then their heads would spin off their necks.

It is up to you as a head to decide what gets through and what doesn't, and this requires a judgement call. Your staff have a finite amount of energy, and you therefore must decide which initiatives they should take on. Sometimes the choice can be difficult, but at other times it is really quite simple. Here, for example, are the key messages from a selection of emails that arrived in my inbox this term (I made one of them up for fun):

* You need to embed the principles of 'intentional design' so that we build a landscape which is coherent, maximizes the enabling benefits of geography and offers an antidote to the challenges of rurality and sparsity. You also need to understand the challenges of social mobility in our Opportunity and Priority areas and start to see the tangible impact of a focused place-based approach. (Two priorities from the South West Regional Schools Commissioner.)

* Teach children how to avoid dog bites, say MPs.

* Don't fail your Ofsted because of one of the six common washroom mistakes schools are making.

* Bivouac building should be taught as part of the national curriculum.

* UKPRNs on GIAS will now be automatically updated when there are changes to the UK Register of Learning Providers (UKRLP). Multi-Academy Trusts (MATs) and other group records now also display a UKPRN. This email is to alert you that one of the governors at the establishment has 180 days until the end of their term. The governing board of

your establishment must ensure that their governance record is correct. If you do not comply you will be terminated.

* My name is Stephen I am interested in being a life model for the art classes for the students am 22 u can call me on 078XXX XXX97 thanks.

Actually, I'm playing with you – the only bit I made up was the bit about being terminated. This is the sort of bilge that comes down the pipe on a daily basis. Luckily, as the school's main filter, I didn't bother anyone with any of this. Just out of curiosity though, I searched the Department for Education's website to see how many documents they had issued during the previous calendar year. I pulled up seventy-five pages each with twenty individual documents, making up 1,500 separate packets of information. The only suitable response to this should either be the ruthless use of the delete button or, if it arrives by post, the instigation of a Mr Gregory-style volcano filing system.

Later this same year, a study from the OECD think-tank, the Teaching and Learning International Survey, looked at the working lives of teachers in forty-eight industrialized countries around the world.

The survey indicated teachers in England worked among the longest hours of any developed countries at fifty hours per week. However, much of this seemed to be administration or other work outside of the classroom.

Despite several attempts by successive governments to reduce teachers' workload, hand on heart, I can honestly say I have not noticed any difference. With a high-stakes school accountability system such as ours, this long-hours admin culture is baked in, and it gets in the way of staff teaching to the best of their ability and keeping our students well.

MAY 2019
LEAVERS' DAY

The Year Thirteen Leavers' Day is a significant moment in the lives of our young people. Once we have got all the predictable and tiresome last-day pranks out of the way, it inevitably turns out to be an emotional morning.

After seven formative years growing up together under the same school roof as friends, classmates and teachers, it is finally time to bring their journey with us to a close. Leaving the safe and familiar for the exciting and new is bittersweet and triggers a genuine tear fest. With old animosities temporarily forgotten, the Year Thirteens rush around hugging each other and getting their shirts signed by friends, foes, favourite and not-so-favourite staff. The leavers' breakfast is followed by musical performances, reviews and emotional thank-yous before the morning culminates in a final rendition of the school song. Then, in a time-honoured fashion, they drift off downtown to the pubs and bars of Torquay. Before they do all of this, I am expected to provide some words of wisdom.

Dear Year Thirteen,

Can you remember your first day at school? Your first lesson, the first time you met your classmates and your teachers? Our first assembly?

Well, I remember being in that assembly and looking out upon a sea of your smiling faces; back then you were keen as mustard, you had name labels sewn in your clothes and pencil cases stuffed full of felt-tip pens. Well, the mustard, the labels and the pens have gone, but it is nice to see that at least some of the smiles remain.

Back then this day seemed impossibly distant, but seven years on here it is, and you are finally at the end of your journey with us. I hope you will look back on your time here with the same affection as we do. I hope you have gained some fond memories, some faithful friends and that, among all the test tubes, trampolines and trigonometry, a spark of passion for your future has been ignited. Any sadness on leaving should be more than compensated by the excitement of looking forward. You have glittering lives ahead of you, and I hope that your experiences here have prepared you well for the future. I know it has not all been plain sailing; we have witnessed your many trials and tribulations, and that is why we are so are immensely proud of the people you have become. It is why we teach. It has been a privilege to watch you grow from wide-eyed lemmings into fine young adults.

This next bit is where I give you some parting advice, and I am conscious that you may well be wondering what useful advice a short, chubby, balding middle-aged man could possibly give you. It's a fair question, but after many years watching students, just like you, pass up through school, I do believe I can offer you a few useful tips. Here they are:

Don't worry if you don't already know what you want to do with your life. Take the time to find your niche. Too many people spend years frantically climbing a ladder, only to find it was leaning against the wrong wall.

Remember, enjoy and relive the compliments you receive. Don't reject them or bat them aside. Suck them in, own them and then proudly say, 'Yes, that's me.' Just not out loud.

Don't mess around with other people's emotions because this can really hurt. By the same token, don't waste any time on people who mess around with yours.

Be an optimist, believe you can determine how your life will be. Have a positive expectancy of your life and regard every setback as temporary.

Look around you at the people in this room. Some you may well never see again, but some will remain your friends for the rest of your lives. Stay in close contact with them, because if the going gets tough in the future, you are going to need them.

Whatever you choose to do in life, be it butcher, baker, candlestick-maker or brain surgeon, never imagine that you are too small or insignificant to make a difference; go out and show the people of Torquay, Devon, the UK and the whole world what you can achieve, then come back here to tell us all the juicy details. You will always be welcome here.

That's it, that's my advice, you can take it or leave it, but after five decades on this planet it's the best I've got. Although you have reached the end of Year Thirteen, and you will no longer physically grace the halls and corridors of TGGS, you will still be with us in spirit. You have left an indelible print on our school, and I don't mean the messages some of you wrote on the exam desks, but a positive imprint on the hearts and minds of the staff here. So, it's not all over. Far from it – it's only just beginning. Our job is done and your future beckons. Go forth and prosper, but before

you do, can I invite you all up onto the stage one
last time, to sing the school song together.

JUNE 2019:
ALRIGHT GUV'NOR!

This term I said a final farewell to Ann White, a long-standing
governor who had been the Chair of Governors at the time
of my appointment. I owed her a lot; not only had she taken
a punt on me, but throughout my headship she consistently
had my back. Alongside this she gave generously of her
time, spending countless hours supporting the school in
meetings, at school events, on interview panels and the like.
I knew I would miss her, and after she left my office for the
last time, I spent a good while reflecting on her selfless and
unheralded contribution to our school.

School governance attracts a colourful spectrum of
people. At one end there are governors who pay an almost
insane attention to policies, documentation, data and details.
At the other end, in stark contrast, there are governors who
never open the documents you spend hours painstakingly
producing, who are on their phones under the table while
you are trying to make serious financial decisions or are
solely interested in getting their daughter her GSCE options
(and are willing to offer you a substantial personal financial
incentive to achieve it).

These extremes of approach often become evident when it comes to staff recruitment, one of the main activities governors get involved in.

During my career I have been involved in appointments where governors have clearly not read any of the application forms or references, do not understand the role they are interviewing for, or have made up their minds before receiving any feedback from the various interview tasks. Sometimes their questioning can fall far short of the forensic grilling required. For example, how they hope to distinguish between candidates with a question like, 'Would you be willing to help out with activities like the Duke of Edinburgh Award scheme?' I don't know. There is only one answer to this type of question and, as far as I am aware, no one has ever said no (myself included). In fact, I've lost count of the number of interviewees who have earnestly claimed that leading students on DfE expeditions happens to be their sole reason for living, only to give some ridiculous excuse as to why they cannot fulfil this vow once they are appointed.

On the other hand, there are some governors who will forensically shift through all of the applications, cross-reference the information and produce copious notes. They can often be attracted to the most obscure details on an application form. At one maths interview, a governor enthusiastically declared, 'I like this candidate . . . look, they've got an HGV licence and are fluent in Croatian.'

I will concede this would be very useful if we suddenly needed someone to drive a truckload of goods to Zagreb, but these attributes are not quite so suited for teaching A-level mathematics.

Because of this variety of approaches, once I became a head I made sure I led the interview process for all of our appointments, as the fallout from a duff appointment can be significant and long lasting.

I have been extremely fortunate with the governors at my current school. Successive chairs and governing bodies have, most of the time, managed to get the difficult balance between support and interference just about right. However, just like many schools, we struggle to recruit and are at the mercy of whoever has the time and inclination to step forward. A situation made worse by the recent DfE strong preference not to have staff serving as governors.

If we are serious about raising the level of school governance nationally, then it cannot be left to the goodwill of a band of 250,000 volunteers. If we want to encourage suitable people to put themselves forward and raise accountability, then chairs and vice chairs should be paid, and the other governors should be entitled to paid time off work to fulfil their duties and attend compulsory high-quality training. You get what you pay for.

In the meantime, I would like to take this opportunity to say to anyone out there toying with the idea of getting involved in the voluntary sector, why not consider becoming a school governor? If you are prepared to adopt the Nolan principles of public life – selflessness, integrity, objectivity, accountability, openness, honesty and leadership – then come on down.

Here are some potted highlights of the governor role at my school. You will be responsible for:

* A £5-million budget: spend it wisely, keep a particularly close eye on the headteacher's expense account and, whatever you do, don't get overdrawn because no one is going to bail you out.

* A motley assortment of 130 staff including an irascible head. You will need to hire them, admire them and occasionally fire them. You are responsible for their wellbeing.

* One thousand students: you need to ensure they are admitted, nurtured, encouraged and at all times kept safe. You must ensure that over their seven years at the school they at least learn something that might be useful to them in the future. Please note they often act like children and don't do as they are told.

* Making sure you are fluent in education-speak and up to date with your acronyms. For example, which two of these are not educational terms: PP, Deep dives, EHCP, Progress 8, PSHE, ESFA,

Skinny dips, Ofqual, ESOL, NEET, EBacc, Extended project, AlOAdOFSHIte?

* Challenging the head on the data. You need to be willing to ask difficult questions such as: can you explain why our P8 score for girls under five foot three inches, called Gertrude, who are taking both textiles and astronomy GCSE, is two points below the average for other seaside towns that begin with the letter T but only have one pier?
* Raising all the complaints, moans and requests you will receive from your friends who have children at the school, once they discover you are a governor.
* Being familiar with the fine detail of all seventy-seven policies including the 'drones over-flying the school' and 'uncollected child' policies.

The material benefits of being a governor are as follows:

* Cash benefits: zero.
* Hospitality: one lukewarm cup of tea and a maximum of two low-grade biscuits per meeting.
* Travel expenses: minimal.
* Other: a great opportunity to work for the good of society and your local community by making a difference to the lives of young people. Please consider putting yourself forward.

SEPTEMBER 2019:
GUT INSTINCT

Alongside processing food, my gut is quite good at alerting me when something is wrong. When I cannot quite put my finger on what is amiss with a situation, but something about it troubles me, I get that nagging, slightly unsettling ache in the pit of my stomach. I ignore this feeling at my peril.

To give students a say in the climate debate crisis, I started a parliamentary petition entitled 'consult with focus groups of young people when creating climate change policy', with the aim of gaining the 10,000 signatures required for the government to respond. To encourage people to sign, we created a video linked to the petition. We filmed the students performing a version of Billy Joel's 1989 hit 'We Didn't Start the Fire', which I had rewritten with green lyrics. The video got over 100,000 views and generated a lot of positive publicity for the cause. Greta Thunberg liked it on Twitter, and we received a handwritten letter of support from David Attenborough. However, it also received some negative feedback. Here's the reply I received from one councillor to whom I sent the video:

Dear Dr Smith,

If you spent more time doing what you are paid to do rather than getting involved in political matters, the world, and particularly the young ladies of Torquay, would be in a much better position to enjoy the world they find themselves in. The clue is in the word 'teacher' in your title. That means to educate. Please think about it rather than clogging up my inbox with your political-biased rubbish.

On the one hand I would love to be able to say, 'I told you so', as the sea laps at her front door, but on the other hand, that would mean we hadn't managed to prevent the icecaps from melting.

A more worrying response came from an agitated local man who was convinced that our girls had become brainwashed by the group Extinction Rebellion. He repeatedly rang reception, and it was very hard to get him off the phone. He was adamant that he needed to discuss the issue directly with me, but despite my gut instinct telling me I really ought to speak with him, I refused to engage.

However, he didn't give up, so one afternoon when he was yet again haranguing Mrs Rumbelow, I told her to put him through. He exploded onto the phone, ranting about his experience with the local leaders of Extinction Rebellion, and how they might be manipulating our girls.

I calmly explained that the group were not involved in our video in any way, but he could not be appeased. Conscious of my next appointment, I tried to end the conversation politely, but unfortunately did so rather clumsily while he was still speaking. I got that familiar feeling in my gut again as I realized that was probably the wrong thing to do and, sure enough, a short time later, the front desk rang to tell me there was an angry man in reception demanding to see me.

He looked menacing, he was clearly very worked up, and, despite my best efforts, I could not calm him down. In fact, all I seemed to do was to wind him up. When I eventually asked him to leave, he became increasingly abusive and suddenly reached inside his overcoat to draw something out. It would be fair to say, given my previous experience, that this was the point at which I cacked myself, but mercifully it was only a phone he withdrew in order to record the rest of our conversation. Just as the receptionist was calling the police, Mr Gregory intervened by escorting him to the front gate and doing exactly what I should have done after his first phone call – he simply listened to what the man had to say. Admittedly this was quite a lot, but as the police never showed up, they had plenty of time. Fifty minutes later the man was satiated, and he left peacefully, content that his concerns had been listened to.

If I had listened to my gut instinct when he had first called, none of this would have happened. Instead, I endured a very stressful afternoon and it was Mr Gregory who had ended up being the hero rather than me.

OCTOBER 2019:
REGARD EVERY SETBACK AS TEMPORARY

In one of our senior team briefings this month, Mrs Browne updated us on the progress of Amanda Heath, one of our former students. Amanda had left the previous year, and her story was a reminder of why we should keep faith in our students even when things look bleak.

Amanda had been a bright, bubbly girl who joined us in the sixth form from another school. Initially things looked like they were going great guns. She quickly integrated with our girls, her subject teachers were very pleased with her work, and she even managed to get herself appointed onto the Head Girl team. In addition to this, she was elected as the Chair of the local hospital's Junior League of Friends, where not only did she raise a large amount of money, but she also recruited many of our pupils to help with their vulnerable-patient feeding programme. This provided the hospital with volunteers and many of our potential medical students with invaluable work experience. On the surface things were looking hunky-dory for this confident and outgoing high achiever.

In reality, Amanda suffered from low self-confidence and her involvement in these activities was her attempt to overcome this feeling. Unfortunately, one consequence of constantly facing her fears was that her anxiety levels remained high. Towards the end of Year Twelve, this anxiety intensified as the AS exams approached. She developed extreme exam anxiety, which involved panic attacks and being physically sick before each exam. Unsurprisingly, this affected her performance significantly, which meant she achieved a set of results that did not reflect her true ability. This knocked her fragile confidence even further and she agonized over the best way forward. After a lot of debate, she took up our offer to re-take the year, hoping we could help her to rebuild her confidence and provide her with some practical strategies to overcome her exam anxiety.

Unfortunately, our intention to boost her confidence was immediately dealt a blow when, due to an administrative oversight, she was omitted from our Year Twelve Awards Ceremony. The following email exchange between myself and her parents reveals their understandable upset, and how our old stalwart Ms Neal helped rescue the situation.

Dear Dr Smith,

Our daughter, Amanda Heath, has not come to school today, as she is very upset.

You will know that Amanda was part of the Head Girl team, she was Chair of the Junior League of Friends, organized the 2015 Christmas fair, frequently attended parents' and open evenings to make refreshments and organized various fundraising events.

Unfortunately, this commitment became too much last year and appeared to be a contributing factor in her disappointing AS-level results, resulting in the need to restart her A-levels.

We were therefore stunned to hear last night that all of the Head Girl team and their parents had been invited to the Award Ceremony to receive an award, but Amanda had not.

Her friends were outraged and embarrassed that she had been excluded. Amanda suffers from confidence issues and associated medical conditions exacerbated by this, yet she throws herself into these voluntary tasks to try and conquer her issues. She was upset that her hard work with the Hospital League of Friends had not been recognized, and even more devastated to hear that the Head Girl team were getting an award and she was not part of that.

Could I ask how this appalling situation has arisen and why such a dedicated, innovative and community-spirited young woman is not recognized?

Dear Mr and Mrs Heath,

I can only apologize profusely that this situation has arisen.

The sixth form team are absolutely mortified by

this oversight, which was likely due to a combination of Amanda changing year groups and the pressures of organizing several significant sixth form events during September. I know this will be of no solace for Amanda. However, over the weekend, I have been putting my mind to how we might reverse this situation and I think I have come up with a solution.

I have managed to speak with Ms Neal (the recently retired Head of Year Thirteen), who had been wanting to leave a lasting legacy at the school after thirty-eight years of dedicated service. I persuaded her to purchase a Dartington glass trophy (it's very impressive) for us to award annually to the individual who best displays 'good citizenship'. She was very taken with the idea and is in complete agreement with me that Amanda would be the perfect first recipient of this trophy. There is also a cash prize attached! She is willing to present the trophy in our Head Girl handover assembly or another suitable event.

Please reassure Amanda that we are genuinely sorry that she was overlooked and that we are determined to rectify the situation.

Best regards,
Dr Smith

This save helped reassure Amanda that we did value her, but it didn't help her anxiety, which grew incrementally as her A-level exams approached. We tried all sorts of strategies to help her. Firstly we asked her to reduce her impressive charity work and focus on herself, then we gave her one-to-one support; we worked on her exam technique and gave her multiple mock exams to help familiarize herself with the process. She was allowed to sit her exams in a separate room to help reduce the anxiety of sitting in an exam hall; she was given extra time, and, alongside this, we referred her to the relevant support services within the school.

Despite all this her anxiety reached such a level that, a few weeks prior to the exam season, she informed us that she didn't feel she was going to be able to come in for any of them. Given all her efforts over the past three years, it would have been an absolute travesty if she was still unable to achieve her potential, and more importantly, it would massively limit her future options. Things were looking pretty desperate.

In the end, the brilliant sixth form team managed to coax Amanda into school for her exams by promising to personally meet her at the school gate, to escort her to her individual exam room, and to sit outside its door for the full duration of each exam. With this physical reassurance, and the strategies we had put in place, Amanda managed to come in and complete all of her exams. On results day in the summer, we were ecstatic to discover she had achieved a fantastic set of results that secured her place at her first-choice Russell Group university.

Mrs Browne had recently spoken with Amanda and was able to give us an update on how she was getting on. It appeared that, with continued support, not only had she been able to manage her exam anxiety at university, and was excelling in her studies, but she had secured a highly competitive and prestigious internship at the UK head office of a luxury automotive manufacturer. Mrs Browne had even invited her in as an inspiring 'old girl' to talk to our students about her experience to show that anything is possible.

This was uplifting news indeed, and when Mrs Browne showed us a picture of a smiling Amanda standing in front of a glitzy automotive stand at a motor show, it reiterated in my mind the parting advice I give in my Year Thirteen leavers' speech: 'Always have a positive expectancy of your future and regard all setbacks as temporary.'

Despite the considerable personal challenge, it now looked like Amanda's setback could end up being just that: a temporary blip in an otherwise sparkling future. We were understandably pleased for her. It is sometimes difficult to get our young people to see that most childhood setbacks, obstacles and disappointments are of a temporary not permanent nature, and that overcoming them is an important part of learning. It is only through adversity that they can develop the grit, determination and resilience essential to navigate life in the twenty-first century. They are certainly going to need it, because Amanda's story was a further reminder of the growing number of students who are routinely developing mental health issues.

This has become a major issue for schools and there had been a significant shift in the focus of our staff over the past decade, so that much more of their time was taken up responding to anxiety issues. The pastoral team were dealing with emotional meltdowns, panic attacks, self-harm, eating disorders and parasuicides on a daily basis. They had become regulars in A&E waiting rooms, on children's wards in hospitals and at crisis meetings with mental health teams. They could be found driving up and down the neighbourhood with police, looking for absconding children at risk of harming themselves. Our students' mental health was subsequently affecting the staff's mental health, as our inability to stem the tide of this growing issue and the effects of dealing with it was highly stressful – we were not trained mental health professionals.

It was all very depressing, and in truth was beginning to get me down a little, a feeling echoed by my fellow heads. The scale of the problem was confirmed by some NHS research, which stated that one in six children aged five to sixteen had a probable mental health disorder: a huge increase from one in nine in 2017. The number of A&E attendances by young people under eighteen with a recorded diagnosis of a psychiatric condition had more than tripled between 2010 and 2019.

Something is wrong; something about our society, our way of life, is not right, and it is manifesting itself in the increasingly poor mental health of our young people. Many reasons have been put forward for this, including:

* Increased parental pressure.
* Increased performance pressure (education, career, financial, etc.).
* A dramatic increase in availability of violent/ sexually explicit material.
* Social media pressure.
* The breakdown of the family unit.
* Confusion or feeling stigmatized over gender or sexual orientation.
* Poor/reduced sleep.
* Increased financial pressure on parents.
* Easy access to, and the acceptance of, recreational drugs.

I don't know what the cause is. I imagine it is most likely to be multi-factorial so, unfortunately, I don't think there are any easy solutions. What is needed is a comprehensive rethink about these many possible contributing factors and the subsequent adoption of some radical national and wholesale healthy changes.

While we wait for our leaders to recognize and respond to this pre-eminent societal issue, we will continue to treat the daily symptoms. Getting our students to adulthood with a healthy mindset has now become our number one priority.

NOVEMBER 2019:
IT WASN'T LIKE THAT IN MY DAY

On open evening, I took a party of parents round the school to give them a flavour of the sort of things our students got up to. One parent kept saying, 'Oh, it wasn't like that in my day', and it is entirely possible that she said this over one hundred times. As the tour progressed, her mantra became increasingly irritating; however, she was not wrong – schools are definitely not the same as when most parents were pupils.

Having once attended school themselves, a number of parents feel sufficiently qualified to advise schools on how best to operate. Of course, everyone is entitled to have an opinion on education, but if you spend a spell in hospital getting your broken leg fixed, you don't then feel sufficiently qualified to advise a surgeon on how to fix your child's broken leg. The same logic should apply to education.

Some parents yearn for a return to the teaching methods of the past, and a few even advocate the reintroduction of the cane, the strap or, that perennial favourite, the good old clip round the ear. The individuals who recommend this often add: 'It didn't do me any harm.' Well, I don't want to appear rude, but that really is a matter of opinion.

Schools have changed to reflect society, so not only would such methods now lead to my imprisonment, but the expectation of schools is so much more than it was in the past. As well as getting students to learn how to read, write and do their sums, we are also responsible for everything else society would like sorted out, from preventing terrorism to stopping children from getting bitten by dogs, from reducing body mass indices to ensuring students can fill in a tax return.

Over the years, the number of parental complaints I receive has risen exponentially, and there is no area of our operation that is not deemed worthy of criticism. Here is a small selection to give you a flavour of the range of complaints.

Arriving at school early one morning, I spied a parent waiting for me in her car. She jumped out, rushed over and repeatedly knocked on my window while I was trying to park. Make no mistake, this is urgent, I thought. Once she had explained to me that she felt her daughter's Year Eight citizenship homework had been unfairly marked, my initial suspicions were confirmed – this really was a genuine emergency. It took about twenty minutes to placate her.

I received a long complaint letter from a parent who was outraged that we had thoughtlessly arranged our New York and ski trips in the same half-term. He was furious that our ineptitude prevented his daughter from going on both, and he wanted me to ring him immediately to explain myself. The letter finished with the immortal line 'it beggars belief'. I rang him, only to receive a tirade of abuse, and despite me explaining that both trips were voluntary, run by staff during their holidays, and that his daughter could go on one trip one year and the other the next, he was still not happy. He seemed strangely disappointed that there was a solution to his problem, and he slammed the phone down in indignation.

We receive multiple complaints about school uniform – usually about the cost, the quality or the style – but I received one complaint from a parent asking me to source uniform with a higher cotton content. She pointed out that the high polyester/cotton ratio (65 per cent/35 per cent) meant that girls felt like they were wearing plastic bags, 'somewhat akin to a boil-in-the-bag cod in white sauce' were her very words. I delegated this one swiftly to our Director of Finance.

I received an agitated email from the parents of one of our girls on a German exchange. The paperwork from the host family listed the father's occupation as 'forester'. Our assumption was that he looked after trees. However, the proper translation was 'woodsman', which in Germany, along with looking after woods, involves a lot of hunting and trapping. As a consequence, the parents were appalled when their daughter sent home pictures of a kitchen full of loaded shotguns and hunting knives. Things became even more untenable when the father came home one evening and casually butchered the boar he had just shot. Covered in blood, he happily scraped out the dead boar's skull in front of her. This was one of many times as a head that I have been accused of failing in my duty of care.

I am also held responsible for many other things beyond my control: freak accidents; natural disasters; unforeseen events; the weather; and acts of God. When these occur, I am again found to be failing in my duty of care and receive communications with familiar opening lines:

'Dear Dr Smith, Do you think it is acceptable . . .'
'Dear Dr Smith, In a direct breach of your policy, you have not . . .'
'Dear Dr Smith, It beggars belief that you have/ have not . . .'
'Dear Dr Smith, You are an absolute lightweight . . .'

The most popular closing sentence is, 'I have copied Ofsted and the press into this letter.' I compare this with the amazing 2018 cave rescue of the Thai football team. The press here in the UK were very focused on why the boys were in the cave, how they had become trapped and to what extent the coach was responsible. In Thailand, which has a 'no blame' culture, they focused on the dedicated coordination of the rescue effort and the notable expression from parents that they did not blame the coach. In fact, they wrote to reassure him of this before the boys were successfully rescued.

Here's the thing. I can sort most things out, most of the time, but sometimes they are beyond my control: the delayed return of the London trip because of the discovery of a World War Two bomb; the canteen running out of gluten-free options one lunchtime; having to call a Snow Day because, of all things, it has been snowing heavily, etc.

It is not a failure in my duty of care – it is just that sometimes things happen, and it is no one's fault. It would be great if, before firing off a wine-fuelled complaint email, parents were to ask themselves, is this someone's fault or is it just an unfortunate turn of events that we can easily move on from?

My feeling is that, most of the time, it is the latter.

Finally, there are a number of parents who are not satisfied with holding me responsible for individual incidents but want to hold me personally responsible that their child has not turned out exactly as they would have wished. I would like to point them towards the following facts:

* Number of hours students are at school under our care per year: 1,365 (16 per cent of the year).
* Number of hours students are at home under their parents care per year: 7,395 (84 per cent of the year).

FRIDAY 20 MARCH 2020:
COVID CENTRAL

On 20 March 2020, all UK schools were closed down in response to the coronavirus pandemic. My daughter, who was returning from university, had developed symptoms of Covid-19, so we decided it would be best for me to isolate myself away from my family until she was no longer infectious.

I did this by moving into a house on the school site that we used as the base for outdoor education. Ensconced here, I managed our on-site provision for key worker children and remotely managed the school staff. I saw this as a chance to finally nail my Hero Head status. However, after several days of rattling around in an empty school, things started to affect me in a way reminiscent of Jack Nicholson in *The Shining*.

I began to write a regular Friday Bulletin for staff in an attempt to keep them informed of what was happening back at the mothership, and to provide them with some light relief. Over the next seventeen months I sent out over fifty of these bulletins. It was only when I reread them recently that I realized how clearly they charted my gradual decline. Here is the first one:

Dear Colleagues,

I hope you are all coping during these unprecedented times. I know that between us there will be 127 very different lockdown experiences, but I'm sure there are some common themes: overuse of funny social media clips; pulling a muscle doing a Joe Wicks workout; or just plain old cabin fever. I myself am in isolation and holed up in Enrichment House (average of 2.0 stars on Trip Advisor from 1 review – mine!).

I've had a few problems settling in. Before the canteen closed down, they supplied me with an industrial-sized tin of baked beans, which I have been steadily working my way through. Even if I don't get the virus there will probably be a real need for a sustained period of self-isolation. Secondly, I borrowed the drama department's toaster. It turns out it's the infamous toaster that set off the school fire alarm last term and is yet to be fixed! Not only have I already burnt two rounds of toast, but it set off the fire alarm again.

The good news is I managed to get myself out onto the paddock and self-registered in under forty seconds – a massive improvement on last time. Buoyed by this success, I tried out our terrorist lockdown procedure, 'Run-Hide-Tell', over the weekend. I must admit there were a few teething problems. I was okay with the running and hiding bits, but the telling bit was difficult because, well, I had no one to tell. I decided to tell myself, but once I had been told, I got quite anxious. I hid in silence under a desk in the physics lab for five hours, but no one came, so in the end I gave up and came out.

I initially counteracted the monotony by walking round and round the grounds, but when I couldn't take it any more, I amused myself by rummaging through all your offices. Very interesting it was, too! Can I ask the owners of the following items to see me on their return – you may wish to consult with your union representative prior to our meeting:

* Homebrew cider kit with three full and two empty flagons of cider.
* A fluorescent orange Mankini.
* The school's missing statue of Caractacus (lost for over a century).

There is some pleasing news: uniform violations, detentions, phone confiscations and incidents of eating in classrooms are all down to zero. I organized several evening house competitions over the last week (i.e. quickest person to run a complete inside circuit of the old building, highest stack of bean bags in the old hall, and the person who has searched the most offices looking for biscuits). I won all of these and hence all the house points go to me.

Here's a list of the events that have happened here this weekend in your absence. I have placed them in order of excitement, with the most exciting last.

* The door to the triangle unexpectedly blew open.
* I tried a ghastly herbal tea in the staffroom.
* One of the seagulls that lives on the roof of the main building attacked me.
* The letter E has fallen off the BEAL house board.
* The caretaker did some painting late Friday afternoon, and I was lucky enough to spend some time watching it dry.
* The clinical waste man woke me up at 6 a.m. on Saturday morning.
* Someone rang me by mistake.
* I have noticed a crack in the plaster on the wall near the main hall that looks a bit like an elephant.

Well, that's all for now, as I have to go. I think something exciting might be happening in the corridor – it looks like one of the lights has started to flicker. I really hope so.

Please stay safe, wash your hands, and I will speak with you all again next Friday.

Dr Smith

The DfE's response to the Covid crisis heralded in a golden age of educational mismanagement. The pantomime villain was the Education Secretary and Frank Spencer look-a-like, Gavin Williamson, who presided over a series of policy U-turns. He was forced to abandon his plans to fully reopen primary schools in the summer term and was twice shamed by Marcus Rashford into extending the free school meals scheme into the holidays. However, his biggest whoopsie on the carpet at Westminster was the exam grade fiasco, where the method used to calculate student grades unleashed hell.

The DfE decided that, with the summer exams cancelled, A-level grades were to be determined by an algorithm that downgraded almost 40 per cent of teacher estimates and reinforced existing inequalities in the system. For example, it meant that the proportion of A*/A grades awarded to fee-paying schools rose by more than double the rate for state comprehensives, and high-performing students at historically low-performing schools were unjustly penalized. This is like being told you have failed your driving test because the people in your neighbourhood usually fail their driving test. Impossible to accept when you didn't even start the car, and just one of many injustices in a system that was untenable. In the face of widespread protest and threats of legal action, Gavin caved in and retracted the algorithm grades in favour of the original teacher estimates, but not before students, schools and universities had been run ragged in the process.

Don't get me wrong – I appreciate that we were in a global pandemic. Many people had already died or lost their jobs and businesses and managing all this must have been extremely tough for the government. The DfE faced a series of major challenges: they were forced to close schools at a moment's notice and reinvent education overnight via a seismic shift to online learning. They had to provide for vulnerable and key worker children, handle the cancellation of summer exams and oversee the safe return of students to school. However, their management of schools throughout this period was characterized by eleventh-hour announcements, policy flip-flops and an impenetrable tsunami of rules, updates, guidance, press conferences and bulletins.

The DfE issued more than two hundred pieces of guidance to schools in the first ninety days of the pandemic, including a dozen days when they issued at least five separate ones. These often arrived at the weekend or at night, and some of them called for immediate action. Trying to interpret and implement this deluge of highly technical and constantly changing advice was overwhelming, especially when we needed real clarity in order to deal with the challenges to come.

First up was the need to divide our site into seven separate physical bubbles before our students returned in September. Arranging the school into this bubble-world meant that each year group could work in its own autonomous bubble, thereby reducing the risk of the virus spreading between the different year groups.

Next, in the spring of 2021, it felt like my career had finally turned full circle. I had to convert our exam hall into a field hospital and train up our staff so that they could administer mass testing to all the students returning to school after the spring lockdown. Staff from across the school willingly mucked in by taking on the different roles required. We had administrative staff guiding students through swab-taking, teachers sanitizing workstations and disposing of clinical waste, and technicians entering results data.

Last but not least, on 4 January 2021, we were informed that once again there would be no summer exams, but that this time, students would be assessed by their teachers. Typically, the guidance from the exam boards on how to assess these Teacher Assessed Grades (TAGs) didn't arrive for another three months, leaving just twelve weeks for teachers to complete this monumental task. The sheer scale of the preparation, implementation, marking and moderation of student work within this short timescale was unprecedented, and caused an enormous amount of assessment angst among teachers and students.

I had begun my headship keen, compliant and eager to please, but over time my attitude towards the educational decision-makers at the DfE and Ofsted, etc. had become increasingly belligerent. Even before the pandemic, the relentless stream of populist policies, half-baked strategies and bungled initiatives had left me punch-drunk. As this interference came in addition to the ongoing funding disputes, the increase in parental pressure and difficulties we had keeping our students healthy, I was battle weary.

By the end of the summer 2020, I had reached crisis fatigue. Headteachers felt like lions being led by donkeys, any remaining faith I'd had left in the competence and integrity of the authorities having been shot through. The final straw came when, randomly searching through my filing cabinet, I came across a newspaper article written about me shortly after being appointed. The person staring out of the page at me looked ridiculously young and optimistic – visibly keen to take on the mantle of headship and the challenges it would bring. The person staring out of the mirror at me every morning did not. I now needed an elasticated waistband in my suit trousers. I wore sensible shoes with cushioned soles, groaned when I got up out of a chair and needed a vat of coffee to get going in the morning. It felt like now would be a good time to pass the baton to someone with fresh eyes and fresh energy.

I decided I would twist and turn to the tune of the DfE no more; Gavin could turn if he wanted to, but here was one old git who was no longer for turning. I resolved to navigate the school through the next academic year – and hopefully see off the worst of the pandemic – before gracefully retiring. As this coincided with the completion of my second stint of seven years at the helm, it seemed to me that the stars were aligned. Therefore, in early September 2020, I handed in my notice to the Chair of Governors and announced my intentions to the staff. A few hundred miles along the coast, Huxley, who I had trained with all those years ago and was now the Executive Head of a multi-academy trust, was doing the same.

Now, it may be my paranoia again, but while the Chair of Governors engaged in what I regarded as a pleasing and appropriate amount of weeping and gnashing of teeth, I swear there was a glint of excitement in her eyes at the prospect of replacing me. In contrast, Caroline, who had already retired, seemed visibly less enthusiastic.

Epilogue: A Call to Arms

Despite all its challenges, lockdown did provide me with the opportunity to properly reflect on my thirty years in education. So, what had become of Project Hero Head? Had I managed to achieve the status I coveted?

Sadly no, nowhere near, really, and the truth is I don't think I ever realistically stood a chance of doing so. I am naturally more of a greying, mild-mannered administrator than a gun-slinging demigod. Only last year a parent mistook me for another parent at an open evening and asked me whether the headteacher was any good. You will be pleased to hear I received a glowing reference and finally got to hear the words 'Dr Smith' and 'hero' in the same sentence.

In the end, I would prefer to be remembered more as an architect, as someone who played the long game and slowly but surely made improvements. Now, at the end of that long game, I find that my educational vision is finally set crystal clear. It's a crying shame it has taken me so long to nail this, as it would have been super-helpful to have felt this assured about it back when I was starting out. However, to salvage something from the wreckage and to ensure my new-found clarity does not go to waste, I will share it with you now.

I believe the primary purpose of schools is to nurture students, so they can make a positive difference to other individuals and to local, national and international communities.

Supporting a friend, being an active member of a local choir, contributing to the economy through gainful employment or raising funds for a global charity – there are an infinite number of ways students can make a positive difference in the world, and therefore the school curriculum must deliver the life skills to facilitate this. The best school motto I have seen in recent years is 'Work Hard, Be Kind'. It says it all really, and if you can instil this in your students, then everything else is a bonus. We must nurture a strong work ethic in our students and point out that the world owes them nothing and that working hard is the best way to improve their life chances. As they bruise easily, they need to learn how to cope with failure, and our aim must be to encourage resilience, to regard all setbacks as temporary, but to know this is a crucial part of the learning process. There is a need for them to develop grit and to cope with things that actively make them want to give up.

We must teach them to manage their emotions and the inevitable stress they will encounter by getting them to ignore things they cannot control, to actively relax and to enjoy the benefits of regular laughter.

They need to learn to be considerate of others (including teachers) by exhibiting good behaviour and observing the boundaries that provide the space for everyone to work productively together.

In terms of learning, we do not want to produce regurgitating robots, so we need to encourage them to question how things are, not to accept them at face value but to critically evaluate and filter the daily torrent of information they receive. They should be exposed to the full range of arts, sciences and humanities. We want them to ponder the very best that human beings have previously thought, said and done in these fields and then go beyond, to imagine how things could be. Taking risks, being creative and innovative are all to be encouraged. We need to create an environment where it is safe to fail, otherwise they will be risk-averse forever, and we must root out 'teenage cynicism' about being keen or clever.

We have a real responsibility to educate the next generation to become outward-looking informed global citizens; they are just as likely to compete with students in Delhi as they are with students in Devon, but more importantly, by understanding different lifestyles, different cultures and different belief systems, they will be more willing to accept them.

We want them to be passionate about things they believe in, but this must be more than waving a banner and liking a tweet. As well as talking the talk, they need to walk the walk by making sure their own behaviours and lifestyle match their views. We need to teach them to clearly articulate and defend these views through informed debate.

Academic achievement is one very important element of education, but it is no more than that – just one of many important elements that together make up a holistic education. Academic success is dependent on students staying healthy, so we need to teach them how to eat a healthy amount of the right foods and how to involve themselves in regular exercise. They must learn how to stay calm and mindful and to get enough quality sleep. They need to be actively involved in their school community, and it is imperative that we make all students feel they belong, while preparing them to move on to the world of work.

They must utilize the positive benefits of technology while being alert to its dangers. And we should be careful to ensure that technology is *used to augment relationships rather than replace them because, as always, the ability to form positive relationships remains paramount. The future of our society depends on our ability to deliver these aims.*

Pie in the sky? Surely these aims are 'noble but absurd, well intentioned but impossible to achieve'? On the contrary, I believe schools are willing and able to deliver on aims such as these if they were not hamstrung by the current education system. We need to be spared the perpetual change spewing out from careerist ministers and to replace our dog-eat-dog results-based landscape with a supportive accountability system.

There is an urgent need to shift our curricular focus onto making sure our students are mentally and physically fit because so many of them are getting ill. This is serious; we are fighting for the future health of our nation.

I can fully understand that having read this book you may well conclude that being a headteacher is simply not worth all the trauma. Well, thankfully you would be wrong, because despite the frustration of government meddling and the need to tweak the nose of adversity on a regular basis, there are many, many glorious reasons why it absolutely is. Here are three recent uplifting examples:

Mr Gregory and I recently exchanged emails with Georgie Hendy, the student caught giving out behaviour slips in our previous school. Mr Gregory had been her English teacher, while I had been in charge of her pastoral care. Georgie, a sliver of a girl from a challenging neighbourhood, had lacked the advantages of many of her peers. Her behaviour was often testing, and she spent more time in my office than anyone else in Key Stage Three. Despite this, I admired her spirit and put her through a student version of the self-esteem course I had attended. Unfortunately, this appeared to make no discernible difference. However, here are the words she wrote to us, all these years later:

Dear Dr Smith and Mr Gregory,

I have been meaning to contact you for a couple of years as I just wanted to say thank you for the support you gave me (and for putting up with me, ha ha) at school.

I'm aware I did not always make the best choices and I could be challenging, but your belief in me had a positive impact on who I am today.

I am a primary school teacher in Cornwall. I teach Year Three and my specialism is English. I've just started my second year after being a teaching assistant for a few years. I thoroughly enjoy it and I want to be the teacher who, like you both, believes in students and helps give them the best opportunities possible.

Apologies for all the time I spent in your offices. I was a defiant teenager, and this is probably the reason why I didn't go down the secondary teaching route myself!

I remember the self-esteem course so well and it is something I have reflected upon especially while doing my teacher training. I am so grateful for the patience and support I received from yourselves and other teachers. Thank you so much! You all played a huge part in my changing path.

Kind regards,
Georgie Hendy

After a seven-month campaign to have their voices heard in the climate change debate, our students secured a meeting with the Business Secretary, Andrea Leadsom MP, at the Houses of Parliament. Six of our students were given forty minutes with the Secretary of State to quiz her on the government's green policies and to put forward their proposal for a student climate summit.

Eloquent, informed, respectful yet challenging, our students were everything we wanted them to be. Andrea Leadsom was a formidable operator, but they gave her a run for her money and made her sit up and listen. The pride I felt in playing even the smallest part in the formation of the minds of these students, our future leaders, was immense.

Finally, we were recently visited by Mrs Pemble who, at 100, was our oldest 'old girl' and the poster girl for our whole-school health curriculum. Despite her advanced age, Mrs Pemble was in rude health; she was mobile with the aid of a stick, lived independently and still delivered a firm handshake. Mentally, she remained quick-witted, humorous and feisty enough to make me slightly nervous.

Because we want our students to live similarly long, healthy and happy lives, we had invited Mrs Pemble to give us her advice on how to do it. She was interviewed by our youngest Year Seven student, and, despite the remarkable eighty-nine-year gap between their respective starting dates at the school, they struck up an instant rapport. Mrs Pemble had worked hard all her life, she had survived the war, she had travelled widely and been a wife and mother. She had trodden the boards for the local amateur dramatic society until well into her eighties and she still tended her beloved garden. She was humble and generous, and the world would be a much better place if there were more people like her in it.

As a teacher, you get the chance to ignite the interest of your students and nurture the future Mrs Pembles and Georgie Hendys of this world. Watching young people grow, achieve their potential, realize their ambitions and turn into responsible young adults is energizing. If you want purpose, to be generative and have a positive influence on the world, then nothing comes close. As a headteacher your reach is even greater, and you can touch, shape and inspire the hearts and minds of future generations. Their future words and deeds will be your legacy.

During the last eighteen months I have seen the very best of teachers; they have stepped up to find a way through the madness and mayhem of the pandemic. They have shown incredible dedication, flexibility and creativity to continue to deliver academic and pastoral care to students in lockdown. They have often been the people holding communities together and a lifeline for struggling students and families.

Virtual learning gave many parents a glimpse of just what teachers do. For the first time, I suspect many had their eyes opened to their dedication, skill and commitment and, if the many letters I have received from parents are anything to go by, this has engendered a new respect for teachers; it is well deserved.

I challenge George Bernard Shaw's witticism, 'He who can does; he who cannot, teaches.' If he were alive today, I would say, 'Oi! Shaw, you come and have a go if you think you're hard enough,' because the reality is that the best doers are often the worst teachers.

For me, teaching fortuitously led to headship and I am so glad it did. Not a day went by when I didn't get to see the talents, skills and enthusiasm of our students and staff, and this brought me a great deal of pleasure. The fact that it may well do the same for you is the main reason for writing this book, and I finish with a call to arms.

I, and others like me, have finally run out of juice, so the profession is predicting a major shortage of headteachers in the near future. Now is the time for others to come forward 'to do something really meaningful'. I urge all potential teachers, and all teachers aspiring to be headteachers out there, to 'come and have a go if you think you're hard enough'. We need people with the belief, hope and humanity to deliver our lofty aims, and if there is one thing I've learnt over the last thirty years, it is that, without doubt, it's well worth all the trauma.

Dr Nick Smith

P.S. I have just received an email that is definitely worthy of a press of the 'beggars belief' monster. I just need to go and find some new batteries.

P.P.S. While I'm at it, I might as well dig out the application form I filled in for that direct entry police superintendent programme.